The

Good Cook's Journal

Other Books by Michele Anna Jordan

The Good Cook's Book of Mustard

The Good Cook's Book of Tomatoes

The Good Cook's Book of Salt & Pepper

The Good Cook's Book of Oil & Vinegar

More Than Meatballs

A Cook's Tour of Sonoma

Vinaigrettes & Other Dressings

The World Is a Kitchen

Lotsa Pasta

VegOut! A Guide Book to Vegetarian Friendly Restaurants in Northern California

The BLT Cookbook

San Francisco Seafood

The New Cook's Tour of Sonoma

Pasta Classics

California Home Cooking

Polenta

Pasta with Sauces

Ravioli & Lasagne

The
Good Cook's Journal

A FOOD LOVER'S COLLECTION OF RECIPES AND MEMORIES

A COMPANION TO THE GOOD COOK'S SERIES

MICHELE ANNA JORDAN

PHOTOGRAPHY BY LIZA GERSHMAN

SKYHORSE PUBLISHING

Skyhorse Publishing books may be purchased in bulk at special discounts for sales promotion, corporate gifts, fund-raising, or educational purposes. Special editions can also be created to specifications. For details, contact the Special Sales Department, Skyhorse Publishing, 307 West 36th Street, 11th Floor, New York, NY 10018 or info@skyhorsepublishing.com.

Skyhorse® and Skyhorse Publishing® are registered trademarks of Skyhorse Publishing, Inc.®, a Delaware corporation.

Visit our website at www.skyhorsepublishing.com.

10 9 8 7 6 5 4 3 2 1

Library of Congress Cataloging-in-Publication Data

Jordan, Michele Anna.
    The good cook's journal : a food lover's record and recipe book / Michele Anna Jordan.
       pages cm
    Includes bibliographical references and index.
    ISBN 978-1-63220-583-4 (alk. paper) 1. Cooking. 2. Cooks—Anecdotes. I. Title.
    TX652.7.J67 2015
    641.5—dc23
                        2015005880

Cover design by Erin Seaward-Hiatte
Cover photo credit: Liza Gershman

Printed in China

for

everyone who has shared my table and invited me to share theirs

•

*the farmers, ranchers, fishermen, winemakers, brewmasters, cider makers, bakers
and chefs who enrich my life daily*

•

the Traverso family and their once and—please!—future market

Contents

Acknowledgments

The Good Cook's Book of Days, as the first edition of this book was called, was inspired by a journal full of menus, guests' signatures and comments, mementos and wine stains that a friend kept near her dining room table. I loved looking through it and recalling the many wonderful meals we shared. Where is that book now, I often wonder? I'm grateful for the memory of it.

Thanks to those long-ago friends for the inspiration.

This new volume was shaped by the frantic pace of photographing dozens of dishes for *The Good Cook's Series* and I'm deeply grateful to photographer Liza Gershman and to Rayne Wolfe, who inspired both Liza and me and the images with her keen eye and fabulous props.

Many thanks to the team at Skyhorse Publishing, especially Nicole Frail, and to my agent, the brilliant Andy Ross, for finding a new home for this book.

And finally, to my family, friends and colleagues, thank you for your patience and understanding of my absence these last many months. I look forward to filling the pages here with new menus, new meals and new celebrations. And soon!

Introduction
to the Second Edition

A few years ago, I was sitting at the bar of a lovely new restaurant in Sebastopol, California, where I live. In the few short weeks it had been open, I'd become a regular, often heading there by myself to enjoy a solo meal. One night, the owner, who was also the chef, sat with me briefly and told me a delightful story.

Before he married, the woman who would become his wife and partner in the restaurant traveled throughout Europe, with a book in which she recorded her adventures. It was an original edition of *The Good Cook's Journal* (then titled *The Good Cook's Book of Days*) that accompanied her. She returned with it full of mementos and tales, delicious ones, I'm certain.

"She'd never tell you," he said, alluding to her soft-spoken nature, and I never mentioned it to her. But whenever I think of it, I smile. It is exactly how I hoped my book would be used, as a vessel for cherished memories.

But do we need such a vessel today, when there's Facebook, Pinterest, Instagram, Snapchat, diary.com, thousands of blogs and countless other ways not just to record moments we want to savor again and again but also to share them?

I believe we do.

Don't get me wrong; I'm no Luddite. I have four functioning Apple computers and an iPhone. I maintain two blogs, a website, am active on Facebook, tweet regularly and have podcasts on iTunes. But none of these supplant the simple joy of opening a book and finding words I've written long ago or a folded menu or torn receipt. Suddenly, there it all is again, right in front of me: the big smile of approval of a passerby as I slurped cold oysters in Paris late one night; a succulent mouthful of seared foie gras and Bing cherry, as sweet as the kiss that would come a bit later; the magic of a crescent moon high in the dark Borneo sky in the early morning, heat rising from the asphalt; a tension-filled dinner—*Go!* the midwife said. *You must eat. There is time*—as we awaited the birth of my grandson Lucas.

Whenever I pick it up, scraps of paper, some stained with droplets of wine, tumble out and, as I tuck them back in, one by one, I recall each moment they represent.

Even so, in light of how we live now, a new edition of a journal had to change. It is so much easier to locate ingredients now than it was in the early 1990s, and easier, as well, to research nearly any topic in the world. Thus I have reduced "The Good Cook's Sources" to a handful of purveyors that I consider essential and expanded the section for noting down your favorite sources. I've made similar adjustments throughout the book, adding web addresses when appropriate and always leading you to what I consider the best ingredient, the best celebration, the best source for whatever it is you love in the wonderful world of the kitchen and the table.

Introduction
to the First Edition

I t was just before Christmas, I think, when I went to dinner at a friend's house. Resting on a sideboard near the dining room table was a large open book of blank pages. Our menu had been written in a fine hand; there was a place for each of us to sign our names, which we did. For the next couple of years, I watched the volume grow, a record of many wonderful afternoons, memorable evenings, special celebrations. I envied that book, the time for such attention to detail that it revealed, the moments of ephemeral pleasures that it captured, the occasional splatter of red wine upon a page. And so, when I am asked why I put together *The Good Cook's Book of Days,* that is the inspiration, the seed from which this little book grew.

I had long searched for a book like this, a beautiful place to record and preserve my day-to-day culinary life, but had failed to find it. How often I've been inspired by a few simple ingredients from the farm market or been struck by some delicious morsel I came across by accident, and how quickly I've forgotten the small details of the moment. Some of my finest gastronomic memories are of casual pleasures I have stumbled upon accidentally: a plum plucked from the tree as I walked down the hill to get the mail, a taco eaten at a roadside stand in Mexico at 7 a.m., bread and olive oil enjoyed in the golden light of an autumn afternoon, a quick meal prepared because old friends stopped by unexpectedly, a glass of wine I never want to forget. I wanted a place to record these details, other than the scribbled notes, random scraps of paper, and occasional printed menu that have served me until now. I will fill in the blanks in this book with great enthusiasm, and when one volume is full, I will start another, assuming that my life continues to be filled with good friends, memorable things to eat and drink, and, of course, the time to enjoy them. Today we are all so busy; this book reveals a wish, a plea, for time to savor the pleasures of life, so many of which emerge around a glass of wine and a loaf of good bread.

What I hope you will do with this is use it as a diary and a journal, a menu planner, an organizer, a resource, but mostly as a source of inspiration. The pages designed for your insertions are meant to entice you, beckon you. The journal section is arranged by seasons, with a listing of the foods of each season, because it seems a sensible way not only to organize this record, but to reinforce that we are cyclical creatures, that we are defined by natural ebb and flow, of changing light and an ever evolving harvest. Many aspects of the modern world conspire to obscure the earth's rhythms; we are now farther removed from the seasons than we have ever been. The interplay of need and abundance, of longing and fulfillment, hunger and satiation, no longer controls our lives. Watermelons—from the southern hemisphere, of course—sit next to cranberries in the fall, apricots appear in the dead of winter, salmon is available year-round. Many find it difficult to recall what is in season, at its peak, when. This book is designed to help you remember.

Once I set out to put this book together, it took on a life of its own, growing into as much of a resource as into a diary. Following the seasonal journal, this book is arranged to help you organize all aspects of your culinary life, from notes about memorable meals and the likes and dislikes of your friends and family, their birthdays and anniversaries, to the phone numbers and addresses of all your favorite stores and restaurants, as well as a couple of pages to record those of stores and mail-order sources that carry your favorite foods. In addition, there are charts and tables offering information on vinegars, oils, mustards, on storage requirements of common pantry items, and on equivalents, along with eight basic recipes to help you put together your own recipes and menus. The sources section lists nearly a hundred businesses and organizations that provide hard-to-find products and information on interesting and unusual culinary festivals; many culinary publications and organizations as well as cookbook stores are also noted.

The archives is a handy repository for details we all forget. Do you loan your cookbooks and then forget who has them? Keep a record of it here and it will be easy to retrieve—or at least to find—that favorite book. And what cook hasn't searched through stacks of books and magazines looking for a favorite recipe whose source has been forgotten? Here, you can record the location of nearly three hundred such recipes so that you can revisit them easily and efficiently. Finally, this journal includes simple recipes, suggestions, tips, quotes, and anecdotes, all intended to assist you in being a good cook and a happy eater.

The Good Cook's Journal of the Seasons

What does eating seasonally mean? This section is designed to help you remember. It is something we all once knew automatically, intuitively, as it was, quite simply, how we lived. If you wanted a peach, you waited until they ripened where you lived. Now nearly everything is available at any time, with apricots, raspberries and tomatoes from the Southern Hemisphere filling our supermarkets in February. Even pomegranates, one of the most stubbornly seasonal fruits, are available all year if you know where to look. I'm not telling because I believe that foods are best in their own true season. This has happened to such an ubiquitous degree that unless you have a reason to pay attention—as I do, because it is both my passion and my work—you probably don't even know when, say, watermelon season actually is. An apricot doesn't taste good in January and not just because an apricot grown to travel long distances must be picked before it has developed its full flavor but also because it's not what our bodies want in the middle of winter. An apricot is a creature of its time, a fleeting pleasure that blossoms in late spring and fades before summer is upon us.

I'm somewhat of a purist when it comes to the seasons but not as strident as I could be. I do not enjoy tomatoes and do not eat them until they ripen where I live but I confess that I find it extremely difficult to be without lemons. I freeze both whole lemons and fresh lemon juice at the peak of the season but I've also resorted to commercial lemons from supermarkets when I run out.

We all make compromises.

In this book, each season has three sections. The first is for menu planning, where you can jot down plans for weekly dinners, school lunches, dinner parties and any other events, with a list of seasonal delicacies to inspire you. Next comes several blank pages where you can record favorite recipes, either by writing them, clipping them and attaching them with tape or by noting a source. Use this section to save suggestions by farmers who grow the produce you buy. Don't know what the funny looking clump that looks like celery from Mars is? It's puntarella; ask the farmer his or her favorite way to prepare it and record it here.

The final section is for your notes and mine. I've included helpful hints, important dates, entertaining quotations and more. You can add your own, along with notes about what inspires you and pleases you about a certain time of year.

A Recipe for Spring

Strawberries and Fromage Blanc

First, you must find really good strawberries, small and sweet as they can be.

Sprinkle the strawberries with a little granulated sugar and set them aside in a cool place for an hour or two.

Mix two cups of your favorite fromage blanc with a tablespoon or two of sugar, a teaspoon of pure vanilla extract, a teaspoon of grated fresh ginger, a tablespoon of finely minced candied ginger, a tablespoon of fresh lemon juice, and a teaspoon of grated lemon zest. Taste and add sugar until it is just right.

Sprinkle a tablespoon of your favorite balsamic vinegar over the strawberries and add a few turns of black pepper. Toss gently to combine the vinegar with the berries' natural juices.

Spoon the cheese into the center of a pretty platter and surround it with the strawberries. Eat it slowly, outside in the gentle spring sun, accompanied by the best champagne you can afford.

Spring Menus

Lunch • Brunch • Afternoon Tea • Spring Equinox • Passover • Easter • Mother's Day Dinner
• Birthday Celebration • Baby Shower • Rehearsal Dinner • Wedding • Birthday Party

Artichokes

Arugula

Asparagus

Baby Leeks

Bamboo Shoots

Better Boy &
Early Girl Tomatoes

Bing Cherries

Blenheim Apricots

Blueberries

Cara Cara Oranges

Chives

Cilantro

Duck Eggs

English Peas

Farm Eggs

Fiddlehead Ferns

First Corn

3

_____   Fresh Fava Beans   _____

_____   Fresh Garlic   _____

_____   Garlic Fronds   _____

_____   Grape Leaves   _____

_____   Green Garlic   _____

_____   Herb Flowers   _____

_____   Herring   _____

_____   Loquats   _____

_____   Morels   _____

_____   Mustard Flowers   _____

_____   Nasturtium Leaves   _____

_____   Nettles   _____

_____   New Potatoes   _____

_____   Pineapple   _____

_____   Porcinis   _____

_____   Queen Anne Cherries   _____

_____   Ramps   _____

_____   Santa Barbara Spot
Prawns   _____

_____   Shad Roe   _____

Soft-Shell Crab

Sorrel

Sorrento Lemons

Snow Brite White
Peaches

Snow Peas

Spinach

Spring Chevre

Spring Lamb

Spring Onions

Spring Salad Greens

Squash Blossoms

Strawberries

Texas 1015
Supersweet Onions

Vidalia Onions

White Asparagus

Wild Mustard Greens

Zucchini

Spring Recipes

The discovery of a new dish does more for human happiness than the discovery of a new star.
—Jean Anthelme Brillat-Savarin, *The Physiology of Taste*

Spring Notes

_____

_____

_____

_____

_____

_____

_____

_____

_____

_____

_____

_____

Mid-March
_____

American Chocolate Week

_____

_____

_____

_____

_____

_____

_____

_____

_____

_____

Asparagus is one of the first joys of spring, arriving, at least in California, a bit before the first strawberries. Instead of boiling or steaming, try roasting asparagus in the oven. Roasted asparagus doesn't need to be peeled, and the process concentrates rather than dilutes delicate flavors. Simply snap off the end of each stalk, put the stalks on a baking sheet, drizzle with just enough olive oil to coat it and season with a little salt and pepper. Roast in a 500 degree oven for 7 to 15 minutes, depending on the size of the stalks. Serve with your favorite sauce or in your favorite recipe, such as asparagus risotto.

*To serve **strawberries** in their own juice, remove their stems, leave whole if small, cut in half if big and sprinkle them with some granulated sugar, not too much. Refrigerate them for an hour or so, during which time the sugar will draw out natural juices. If you have too many berries to enjoy at once, this will give you an extra day or two. Just keep them covered and chilled.*

Late March or Early April
World Catfish Festival, Belzoni, Mississippi

_____
_____
_____
_____
_____
_____

Last Full Week in April
World's Biggest Fish Fry, Paris, Tennessee

_____
_____
_____
_____
_____

Today before a goblet of wine I was shamed, My third cup unfinished, I couldn't pour another. Wondering why I am always drunk beneath the flowers, Perhaps the spring breeze has made me tipsy.

—Yüan Chen, ninth century

_____
_____
_____
_____
_____
_____

Salt improves the taste of almost everything, drawing the disparate elements of a dish together, unifying them, and, because it dissolves slowly on the tongue, contributing to the harmonious blending of flavors and creating a pleasing finish on the palate. Salt: It is flavor's midwife and no cook should be without it. There are many types, today nearly as many as there were around the turn of the nineteenth century. Try flake salt, the grains of which scatter across the tongue and melt like tiny stars, enchanting and mysterious, like taste itself.

Last Weekend in April

Vermont Maple Syrup Festival;
Asparagus Festival, Stockton, California

April

National Florida Tomato Month, National BLT Month,
National Grilled Cheese Month

To crave and to have are as like as a thing and its shadow. For when does a berry break upon the tongue as sweetly as when one longs to taste it, and when is the taste refracted into so many hues and savors of ripeness and earth, and when do our senses know a thing so utterly as when we lack it? And here again is a foreshadowing—the world will be made whole. For to wish for a hand on one's hair is all but to feel it. So whatever we may lose, the very craving gives it back to us. Though we dream and hardly know it, longing, like an angel, fosters us, smoothes our hair, and brings us wild strawberries.

—Marilynne Robinson, *Housekeeping*

_____

_____

_____

_____

_____

_____

_____

First Week In May
National Herb Week

_____

_____

_____

_____

_____

_____   *To preserve flavor, store **olive oil** in a cool,*
dark pantry, not in the refrigerator where its
delicate flavors will be destroyed, nor next to
the stove, where heat will have the same effect.

_____

_____

_____

_____

_____

_____

_____

_____

_____

_____

_____

*Here's a little secret about spring. If you live close to a cultivated **asparagus** patch, take a look around a few weeks after it comes into season. Keep your eyes open for a slender green stalk, and if you find one, look for more. It will be the highly prized wild asparagus, an escapee from its cousin's more mannered environment. It is delicious: sweeter and more tender than the domesticated variety. Many aficionados prefer to eat wild asparagus raw to fully savor its delicacy.*

Cherries are the first of summer's fruit, absolutely delicious in their own right, but also an intimation of what is soon to come. They have a painfully short season, which leads to a certain sense of urgency when they first appear. Better hurry, better eat as many as possible before they vanish. A fresh sweet cherry is irresistible; the rest of the year, use dried cherries, which are quite wonderful, especially with smoked poultry.

As the winter snow melts and days grow warmer, the first of the year's **mushrooms**, *the tantalizing morels, poke through the ground. Hunt for them in forests and meadows, especially near last year's forest fires, but do be sure you know exactly what you are looking for. If you have the slightest doubt, consult an expert. Morels fruit through early June. Add them to a soup or stew or enjoy them simply, sautéed in a little butter, seasoned with salt, pepper, and brandy, and finished with a little heavy cream.*

The kitchen, reasonably enough, was the scene of my
first gastronomic adventure. I was on all fours. I crawled
into the vegetable bin, settled on a giant onion, and ate
it, skin and all. It must have marked me for life, for I
have never ceased to love the hearty flavor of raw onions.
      —James Beard, *Delights and Prejudices*

Mid-May
International Pickle Week

May 24
Anti-Saloon League founded, 1893

Grilled **green onions** are common at roadside taco stands throughout Mexico, and easy to duplicate at home. Simply rub a bunch of cleaned scallions (about 12) with a bit of olive oil and roast them in a 375 degree oven or grill them on a stove-top grill until they are limp and tender. Serve wrapped in a warm corn tortilla or with steamed rice and plenty of your favorite salsa. You can prepare baby leeks in the same way.

To make a simple yet versatile and delicious **mustard cream**, mix together 1¼ cups crème fraîche (or 1 cup sour cream thinned with ¼ cup half-and-half) with ¼ cup Dijon mustard, 1 teaspoon kosher salt, and 1 teaspoon freshly ground pepper. You can use it immediately or refrigerate it up to 10 days. Serve as a dip with vegetables or prawns; as a topping for split pea soup; as a dressing for potato salad, grated celery root, or avocados filled with smoked chicken and fennel; or alongside grilled or broiled fish, carpaccio, pate, or roast beef.

Third weekend in May
World Championship Barbecue
Cooking Contest, Memphis, Tennessee

May
National Strawberry Month

Bats, perhaps the most misunderstood animals on the planet, are essential pollinators of a huge variety of plants, including many delicious foods both in the United States and throughout the world; over 450 cash crops—mangos, guavas, dates, figs, and avocados, for example—rely upon bats' natural activity to reproduce and, sometimes, to survive. As the only nocturnal flying predators of insects, bats perform a fundamental task as they go about their nightly meal, reducing not only mosquito populations, but also other harmful pests that left unchecked would decimate important crops. Bats, whose more than one thousand species make up 25 percent of all the earth's mammals, are among the longest-lived (up to thirty years) animals for their size, are not related to rodents, and are extremely intelligent. They were, originally, classified as primates until the order of Chiroptera, which means "hand wing" was established. Without bats, the ecological balance of the planet would be shattered.

Gawai Dayak is celebrated in the Malaysian state of Sarawak on the island of Borneo on May 31 & June 1. The festival gives thanks for a plentiful rice harvest. A month before the festival, the brewing of tuak—rice wine—begins, using a variety of glutinous rice. When visitors join in the festival, they are expected to accept—and drink!—a glass of tuak from each family of the longhouse where they are celebrating. (Longhouses are like rustic, horizontal apartment buildings, with a large common area to escape the heat of the day and to share in such celebrations as this one.) It is typical for longhouses to have as many as a hundred "doors"—think apartments—and more and so you can just imagine the stories of overconsumption shared by those who have made it back from Gawai Dayak.

_____

_____

_____

_____

_____

_____

_____

_____

_____

_____

_____

_____

_____

_____

_____

_____

_____

_____

_____

_____

_____

Apricots come into full season quickly and do not linger for long. If you don't pay attention, you can miss them entirely. To capture their flavor, make apricot chutney. In a large, heavy pot combine 5 pounds apricots (halved, stones removed) with 3 pounds sugar, 1 pound currants, 1/2 cup minced fresh garlic, 7 serranos (stemmed and cut into thin julienne), 5 ounces fresh minced ginger, 1/2 ounce dried hot chilies, 3 cups apple cider vinegar, and 2 tablespoons kosher salt. Stir until the sugar is dissolved and then simmer over low heat for about an hour. Ladle into sterilized pint or half-pint jars and process in a water bath for 15 minutes. You can make a similar chutney with summer peaches.

A Recipe for Summer

Aioli

To make aioli, peel a handful of fresh garlic, preferably from a friend who's grown it. Place the cloves in a large stone mortar and add a teaspoon of kosher salt.

Have two cups of olive oil (provencal, tuscan, ligurian or californian) nearby.

Using a wooden or stone pestle, pound the garlic into a liquidy pulp. Add a deeply colored egg yolk from a hen allowed to run free, and then add another egg yolk, gently mixing with the pestle.

Begin to pour a thin trickle of olive oil into the side of the mortar, beating with the pestle all the while. Continue until all the oil has been incorporated. Taste the aioli and if it is a bit flat, add a little more salt dissolved in a teaspoon of lemon juice. Mix it in.

Smear the aioli on toasted slices of baguettes, set them into bowls and spoon flavorful bouillabaisse broth over them. Though not traditional (for that you must make rouille), this is very, very good. Pass platters piled high with the fish, mussels, crabs and potatoes of the bouillabaisse.

Have plenty of chilled dry roséat the ready.

If you can, do this in the south of France near the sea, where the sky is the color of periwinkles and the light liquid and buttery.

Summer Menus

Fourth of July Barbecue • Camping • Picnic • Beach Party • Clam Bake • Midsummer Night Supper
• Solstice Celebration • Birthday Party • Labor Day

Arctic Gem White
Peaches

Armenian Cucumbers

Avocados

Bartlett Pears

Bell Peppers

Black Truffles

Blackberries

Blue Lake Green
Beans

Blueberries

Bosc Pears

Cantaloupe

Chard

Charentais Melon

Cinnamon Basil

Comice Pears

Concorde Pears

Corn

Crenshaw Melon

Duck Eggs

Elephant Heart
Plums

English Cucumbers

Fay Alberta Yellow
Peaches

Fantasia Nectarines

Farm Eggs

French Breakfast
Radishes

Fresh Chickpeas

Garlic

Golden Chanterelle

Gooseberries

Gravenstein Apples

Green Tomatoes

Gypsy Peppers

Haricots Verts

Hedgehog
Mushrooms

_____ Heirloom Tomatoes _____

_____ Honeydew Melon _____

_____ Howard Miracle
Plums _____

_____ Jalapeños _____

_____ Lavender _____

_____ Licorice Basil _____

_____ Lemon Cucumbers _____

_____ Mango _____

_____ Mulberries _____

_____ Nasturtium Flowers _____

_____ Nectarines _____

_____ Okra _____

_____ Opal Basil _____

_____ Papaya _____

_____ Peaches _____

_____ Pickling Cucumbers _____

_____ Poblanos _____

_____ Pluots _____

_____ Queen Anne
Cherries _____

————————   Raspberries   ————————

————————   Red Bartlett Pear   ————————

————————   Rhubarb   ————————

————————   Santa Rosa Plums   ————————

————————   Serranos   ————————

————————   Shaggy Mane
Mushrooms   ————————

————————   Shallots   ————————

————————   Sharlyn Melon   ————————

————————   Squash Blossoms   ————————

————————   Sungold Cherry
Tomatoes   ————————

————————   Sweet Basil   ————————

————————   Thai Basil   ————————

————————   Walla Walla Onions   ————————

————————   Watermelon   ————————

————————   Wild Pacific King
Salmon   ————————

————————   Zucchini   ————————

Summer Recipes

Summer Notes

June
National Dairy Month

"Basil should not be planted," my dear friend and colleague Frederique Lavoipierre says, "until it is warm enough to lie on the ground outside, naked." **Basil**—its fresh, evocative scent, its compelling flavor—has become synonymous with summer. Don't let the season pass without stocking up on homemade pesto, made not in a blender or food processor but crushed by hand in a large mortar or suribachi.

39

The best way to peel a tomato is to pierce it—through its blossom end—onto the tines of a fork and scorch the skin over a gas flame. Turn the fork quickly so that the flesh doesn't begin to cook; it will take 5 to 15 seconds per tomato, depending on size. A boiling-water bath does loosen the skins, but it also dilutes the tomato's flavor.

July 3
M F K Fisher born, 1908

July 14
Bastille Day; Chez Panisse Garlic Festival, Berkeley, California

*Slice ripe **peaches** or nectarines, sprinkle a little sugar over them, followed by a squeeze of lemon juice and a splash of muscat wine. Serve chilled.*

Never refrigerate a raw tomato. Store at temperatures above 55 degrees and use within 3 to 4 days. To save tomatoes about to turn, chop them and cover them with vinegar or olive oil. Then store in the refrigerator and use within a day in a sauce, salsa, or vinaigrette.

_____

_____

Second week in July

National Cherry Festival, Traverse City,
Michigan, the "Cherry Capital of the World"

_____

_____

_____

_____

_____

_____

_____

_____

Third weekend in July

Pork, Peanut, and Pine Festival, Surry, Virginia

_____

_____

_____

_____

_____

_____

_____

_____

_____

_____

_____

For delightful (and healthy) summer desserts, grill fruit over the cooling coals of a barbecue. Fresh apricot halves take about 3 minutes on each side; serve them with a squeeze of lime juice and a little brown sugar. Peaches, cut in half, take slightly longer until they are heated through and just tender. After removing them from the grill, spoon into their centers fresh goat cheese (fromage blanc) that you have mixed with a bit of vanilla, sugar, grated fresh ginger, candied ginger, and lemon juice.

Last weekend in July
Gilroy Garlic Festival, Gilroy, California

When one has tasted watermelons, one knows what angels eat. It was not a Southern watermelon that Eve took; we know it because she repented.
—Mark Twain

In the south of France, **new garlic** is celebrated with an Aioli Monstre, a feast during which the freshest vegetables, hard-cooked eggs, poached salt cod, stewed octopus, bread, and plenty of red wine are served with aioli, a robust garlic mayonnaise. It's an easy meal to create yourself. Simply use the year's first garlic to make a powerful aioli, at least a full head per cup of olive oil. If you don't want to bother with poached salt cod and stewed octopus, serve roast leg of lamb.

In June, the first of summer's corn coincides with the last of the year's **cherries**. Capture the moment in a cherry & corn salsa, delightful with gravlax or fresh grilled salmon. Toss 1 pound Bing cherries, cut in half and pitted, with about a cup and a half of very fresh corn kernels, quickly cooked and then cut from the cob. Add 2 chopped shallots, 1 chopped jalapeño pepper, 2 teaspoons finely chopped mint, a teaspoon fresh thyme leaves, 3 tablespoons unrefined corn oil (or olive oil), 2 tablespoons medium-acid vinegar (cherry, raspberry, or sherry), and ½ teaspoon kosher salt. Let rest for 30 minutes before serving.

_____

_____

July

*National Blueberries Month; National
Watermelon Month; Jasmine flowers in full bloom*

_____

_____

_____

_____

_____

*Should you be lucky enough to find yourself with an abundance of summer **berries**—raspberries, blackberries, blueberries—preserve their essence in homemade fruit vinegar. Add twice as much fruit as white wine vinegar to a glass jar or crock, cover, and store in a cool cupboard or refrigerator for 2 to 10 days, tasting regularly to determine when your berry vinegar is sufficiently flavored. Strain it through cheesecloth or a paper coffee filter, bottle your vinegar, and store in a cool, dark cupboard. You can make peach, nectarine, or apricot vinegar by the same method.*

Take advantage of the sun's free energy to make sun tea. Just fill a glass jar or pitcher with water, add the tea, and place it in the sun for an hour or two, until the tea is as weak or strong as you prefer. Chill and serve over ice.

First weekend in August
International Pinot Noir Festival,
McMinnville, Oregon

August
National Peach Month

August 5
National Mustard Day

Ripe, tangy **tomatoes**: *summer's pride. Enjoy them now, and let them be just a memory during the months when they taste like little more than soggy cardboard. For a simple dish, peel 4 medium tomatoes and cut them into wedges. Heat a little olive oil in a sauté pan and cook the tomatoes quickly, about 2 minutes on each side. Season with a squeeze of lemon, salt, and black pepper; scatter minced scallions over them or top them with some finely minced garlic and very thin strips of basil. Serve immediately as a side dish, with some chèvre and good bread alongside.*

August 8
Sneak Some Zucchini onto Your
Neighbors' Porch Night

For a refreshing late-summer snack, place a bunch or two of **grapes** *(organic, please!) in the freezer until they are frozen solid. They are great on swelteringly hot days, and kids love them.*

August 15
Julia Child born, 1912

August 17
Watermelon Festival, Hope, Arkansas

One of the simplest pleasures of summer is a salad of sliced tomatoes, variations of which are nearly endless. To serve 4, slice 4 large tomatoes through their equators—horizontally, not vertically—arrange them on 1 large or 4 small plates, drizzle with extra-virgin olive oil, and sprinkle with a little flake salt and freshly ground pepper. Dress up the salad with minced Italian parsley and garlic, grated cheese, fresh basil and slices of mozzarella fresca, thin slices of Meyer lemon, anchovy fillets, sliced olives, or tinned sardines and thin slices of onion.

A Recipe for Fall

Eat Daily from August until the First Winter Storm

A loaf of good, hearty bread
Tomatoes fresh from the garden and warm from the sun
The best extra-virgin olive oil you can find
Malden salt flakes
Black pepper in a mill
A glass of red wine

Tear off a chunk of bread and place it in a hot oven. Slice the tomatoes into thick rounds and lay them on a plate. Drizzle with a little olive oil and sprinkle with salt and pepper. Get the bread from the oven, pour olive oil all over it and then add some salt and pepper.

Take your bread, tomatoes, and glass of wine outside or to the nearest westward window. Watch the light change.

Fall Menus

School Lunch • Rosh Hashanah • Harvest Feast • Harvest Moon Celebration • Makahiki Luau
• Halloween • Dia de los Muertos • Thanksgiving • Birthday Party • Wedding Shower • Retirement Party

Arkansas Black Apples

Artichokes

Arugula

Asian Pears

Beets

Belgian Endive

King Bolete Mushrooms

Broccoli

Brussels Sprouts

Buddha Hand Citron

Cauliflower

Chestnuts

Chocolate Persimmons

Cranberries

Edamame

Eggplant

Escarole

Fall Salad Greens

Fennel

Forelle Pears

Fresh Dates

Fuyu Persimmons

Green D'Anjou Pears

Habanero Chilies

Hazelnuts

Huckleberries

Italian Frying Olives

Jonathan Apples

Last Chance Yellow
Peaches

Maitake (Hen-of-the-
Woods) Mushrooms

McIntosh Apples

Olives

Pomegranates

Popcorn on the Cob

Pumpkins

Quince

Radicchio

Red D'Anjou Pears

Sage

Savoy Spinach

Seckel Pears

Starkrimson Pears

Sweet Potatoes

Table Grapes

Taro

Tomatillos

Walnuts

Watermelon

Winter Squash

Wine Grapes

Fall Recipes

Fall Notes

_____

_____

_____

_____

_____

_____

_____
                                            September
_____
                          Cranberry Festival, Bandon, Oregon;
_____
                          National Organic Harvest Month

_____

_____

_____

_____

_____

Weekend following Labor Day
_____
Castroville Artichoke Festival, Castroville, California

_____

_____

_____

_____

_____

_____

_____

_____

_____

_____

_____

Beets are available year-round but are at their natural peak in late summer and early fall. In addition to the familiar red beet, there are several other varieties, all absolutely delicious. Look for golden beets, white beets, and the red and white striped beets called Chioggia. Rather than boiling them, concentrate their flavors by roasting them whole in the oven. Rub trimmed, unpeeled beets with a little olive oil, place them on a baking rack in a 350 degree oven and roast until tender, from 45 to 90 minutes, depending on size. Remove them from the oven and allow to cool before peeling them. Serve them cut in quarters and tossed with toasted walnuts, crumbled Roquefort cheese, a splash of olive oil, and plenty of fresh ground pepper.

*To preserve a piece of fresh **ginger**, place it whole or sliced in a jar and cover it with rice wine vinegar. Slice off or remove pieces as you need them. Use the vinegar too, which will be evocatively perfumed with the aroma of ginger. Stored in a cool, dark cupboard, both the ginger and the vinegar should keep for about a year.*

Mini-pumpkins *make colorful decorations, but they are also delicious to eat. Bake them in a 350 degree oven until they are tender, about 40 minutes (or punch a few holes in them and cook in the microwave for about 10 minutes), cut off the stem ends, scoop out the seeds, and fill with your favorite risotto or several cloves of roasted garlic.*

Mid-September

National Heirloom Exposition, The World's Pure Food Fair, Santa Rosa, California.

September 26

Johnny Appleseed born, 1774. Johnny Appleseed did not travel the country planting seeds for pie. He planted seeds for hard apple cider, once the most common beverage in America, enjoyed throughout the day by people of all ages, including children. It was considered more pure and more healthful than water.

*To dry **chilies** at home, thread them through their stems on string and hang them several feet above a wood stove until they are dried. Store them in the pantry or the kitchen and remove them as needed.*

Second weekend in October

Gumbo Festival, Bridge City, Louisiana

The olive tree is surely the richest gift of Heaven.
    —Thomas Jefferson, *letter to George Wythe*

Although ***figs*** *come into season beginning in late spring, by fall there is an urgency to their abundance. A fresh fig has a brief life and moves quickly from its soft yielding appeal to collapse and decay. Keep figs for only a day or two in the refrigerator. To make a simple fig chutney, purée 10 ripe figs with 3 cloves garlic, 1 to 2 tablespoons lemon juice, 1 teaspoon kosher salt, 2 teaspoons toasted and crushed cumin seed, ½ teaspoon red pepper flakes, and ½ cup water. Store in the refrigerator and serve as a condiment with yogurt, curries, roasted meats, and poultry.*

October 8–15
American Beer Week

September–October
Oktoberfest celebrations held all over the world

October 12
National Dessert Day

In Latin America, Día de los Muertos—Day of the Dead, from which our Halloween has evolved— is celebrated on November 1 and 2. Graves and entire cemeteries are decorated, and altars are built to honor departed loved ones, who, according to tradition, return to partake of the sensual pleasures of the flesh that are denied them in the spirit world. Loved ones' favorite dishes along with traditional foods like panes de muertos, a sweet, dark bread flavored with anise and baked in human and animal shapes, are added to the altars. In a particularly touching gesture, many Mexican families hang baskets of traditional foods outside their homes so that passing spirits without families or friends will have something to eat.

*When you purchase **vinegar**, be sure to check the level of acidity, expressed either as a percentage as in, say, 6 percent, or in grain, as in 60 grain. The higher the number, the greater the amount of acetic acid and the stronger the vinegar will be. For general cooking, 5.5 to 6 percent is best. Higher, and other flavors may be eclipsed.*

October

International Association of Culinary Professionals' Cookbook Month; Pumpkin festivals held throughout the country

Medieval people ate between 10 and 20 grams of salt a day, far more than the average modern American. . . . On the table, salt was kept in salt cellars, elaborate contraptions of precious metals, often sculpted into shells, dragons, or ships as high as two feet. They became most important utensils, embodying not only expense and artistry, but the potency of salt's supposed magic, its ability to spread evil if mishandled, bring luck if treated with care. Cellars were symbols of wealth, status, and superstition. The salt itself was carefully piled in the center—perhaps in the hold of a perfect ship with eight miniature crewmen—and rounded into a small white mountain.

—Sallie. Tisdale, "Lots Wife"

Fresh **fennel** has a delightfully delicate, fragrant flavor. It is outstanding cut in half, browned, and then braised until tender in olive oil and white wine. It is equally delicious shaved very thinly, tossed with extra-virgin olive oil and fresh lemon juice, and served with thin curls of Parmigiano cheese scattered over the surface.

Last Sunday in October
Saffron Rose Festival, Consuegra, Spain

Late October, every other year
Slow Food's Terra Madre and Salone del Gusto, the world's largest food and wine fair, Torino, Italy

The first of the year's olives are harvested in California and in Europe, and the new olive oil is pressed.

Tapenade, *a paste of olives, anchovies, garlic, and various other ingredients, is a versatile and enticing condiment. It can be combined with a good mayonnaise for a sandwich spread or thinned with olive oil and a bit of warm water for a simple pasta sauce. It is excellent as a garnish with baked goat cheese and delicious served with hot bread. To make a simple tapenade, purée together ½ cup pitted Kalamata olives, 2 or 3 cloves garlic (peeled), 2 or 3 anchovy fillets, 1 tablespoon Dijon mustard, 1 tablespoon minced fresh Italian parsley, and ½ cup extra-virgin olive oil. Store in the refrigerator for up to 10 days.*

October 31

All Hallows' Eve

Pomegranates *are the first, and arguably the most beautiful, of fall fruits. They also disappear quickly, though not as quickly as they once did, thanks to a producer in Southern California who has pushed their season, with the first usually appearing in November and the last in January or February.*

November 1

El Dia de Los Muertos

Most commercial flavored oils are, in spite of their current popularity, a waste of money (sad but true); even those made at home are of limited value. If you must, make them with room-temperature, good-quality olive oil, blanch and dry fresh herbs before using them, and make the oil in small quantities that will be used within a day or two. Homemade flavored oils must be refrigerated.

*Regardless of when you purchase them, most mature **potatoes** are harvested from September through November. Potatoes keep well, provided they are stored properly, between 45°and 50°F and away from light. Onions prefer these conditions, too. But never store the two vegetables together; each gives off a gas that shortens the life of the other.*

Cranberries are harvested in the fall and begin appearing in the marketplace in late September and early October. Cranberry vinegar makes a dazzling holiday gift and is very easy to prepare. Chop cranberries in a food processor and for each 4 cups of berries, add 2 cups of white wine vinegar. Let the mixture sit in a glass jar or crock, covered, in a cool pantry or refrigerator for about a week. Strain through several layers of cheesecloth or a paper coffee filter. Pour the cranberry vinegar, which will be the color of liquid rubies, into slender bottles of clear glass. Add a long thin twist of orange zest or several fresh cranberries threaded on a wooden skewer to each bottle and close with a cork. Store in a cool dark cupboard until ready to use.

November 12–19
National Culinary Week

November 15
National Clean Out Your Refrigerator Day

Third Thursday in November
*The fall's new vintage of Beaujolais
Nouveau is released in France.*

Sweet potatoes, *native to America and members of the morning glory family, are delicious baked in the oven, sliced in lengthwise wedges, baked again, and then drizzled with a bit of your favorite vinaigrette. They are also packed with good-for-you substances, including vitamin A (more than almost any other food) and antioxidants, which are said to slow the aging process and prevent cancer.*

A Recipe for Winter

Tomato & Bread Soup

On a cold night when you need the quick comfort of good soup, try this one, a traditional Italian bread soup full of simple good flavors.

For four people, sauté a handful of peeled and chopped garlic in olive oil. Add four cups of diced tomatoes—those that you canned a few months earlier are ideal—and simmer for five minutes. Add four cups of chicken stock, return to a simmer, add several turns of black pepper and kosher salt to taste.

Have three cups of bread cubes, torn from crusty, coarse-grain, day-old hearth bread into uneven pieces—divided among four bowls. Ladle the soup over the bread and let it sit for five minutes so that the bread soaks up some of the juices. Just before serving, drizzle a tablespoon or two of extra-virgin olive oil over the soup and scatter a nice bit of chopped Italian parsley on top. Add plenty of freshly ground black pepper.

Eat this by a roaring fire, with good friends gathered around you and a cat asleep on the hearth.

Winter Menus

Chanukah • Christmas Eve • Christmas Breakfast • Birthday Party • Christmas Dinner • New Year's Eve • New Year's Day Brunch • Epiphany • Valentine's Day • Mardi Gras

Belgian Endive

Black Chanterelles

Blood Oranges

Broccoli

Brussels Sprouts

Burdock Root

Cabbage

Cara Cara Oranges

Cardoons

Cauliflower

Clementines

Celery Root

Dungeness Crab

Eureka Lemons

Frisee

Hachiya Persimmons

Horseradish

Jerusalem Artichokes

Kiwifruit

Kumquat

Lacinato Kale

Meyer Lemons

Mustard Greens

Oysters

Parsnips

Puntarella

Pomelo

Rutabaga

Salsify

Sarawak Grapefruit

Sunchokes

Tangerines

Turnips

White Truffles

Winter Salad Greens

Yacon

Yukon King White
Peaches

Winter Recipes

Winter Notes

November 22

French chef and author Madeleine Kamman's birthday

To make **crème fraîche**, *scald a pint glass jar and its lid with boiling water. Dry it thoroughly, add 1 or 2 cups heavy cream and 2 or 3 tablespoons cultured buttermilk. Close the jar and shake it for about 30 seconds to mix it well. Set it in a warm place—about 70°F is ideal—for around 24 hours, until it is thick. Stir well and refrigerate. The crème fraîche will keep for about 10 days.*

HOW TO CURE A COLD: *One tall silk hat, one four poster bed, one bottle of brandy. To be taken as follows: put the tall silk hat on the right-hand post at the foot of the bed, lie down and arrange yourself comfortably, drink the brandy, and when you see a tall silk hat on both the right and left bedposts you are cured.*

—*An old French proverb, in* M. F. K. Fisher, *A Cordiall Water*

Rosemary *is a hearty—and deliciously fragrant—herb that grows easily and abundantly. If you live in a warm climate without harsh winters, plant it directly in the ground. Otherwise, plant your rosemary in a pot that you can bring inside for the winter. When you need a little for a recipe, simply snip off a sprig.*

December 5
Prohibition ended, 1933

December 22
California Kiwifruit Day

Nothing is so effective in keeping one young and full of lust as a discriminating palate thoroughly satisfied at least once a day.
—Angelo Pellegrini, *The Unprejudiced Palate*

For a delicious winter salad, peel and slice several oranges (blood oranges, if you can find them) and arrange them on a plate. Drizzle with the best Italian olive oil you can find and then add a bit of kosher salt and several turns of black pepper in a mill. Use a vegetable peeler to shave off thin strips of Parmigiano or Romano cheese and scatter the strips over the oranges. Serve with winter greens alongside and a light-bodied red wine.

Potato soup is a delicious winter staple. If you can make it on top of a wood-burning stove, so much the better, but any source of heat, even a hot plate in a tiny apartment, will do. just sauté a couple of yellow onions in some olive oil until they are very soft. Add 4 or 5 russet potatoes (about 3 pounds, scrubbed and diced) and cover it all with 8 cups stock, water, or a combination of both. Simmer until the potatoes are tender, about 20 minutes. Purée with an immersion blender, season with salt and pepper, and add whatever else you like: 3 cups grated Cheddar cheese, chopped fresh spinach sautéed in olive oil and garlic, sautéed garlic and a can of diced tomatoes, a puréed chipotle pepper and spicy sausages, 3 cups cooked broccoli.

December

Congress adopts the Volstead Act to enforce the Eighteenth
Amendment, prohibiting the manufacture, sale, transportation,
import, or export of alcoholic beverages, 1919

Oysters are the Champagne of shellfish.
—Herb Caen, *June 1, 1987*

January 6

Feast of the Epiphany, oldest Christian holiday (also celebrated as Twelfth
Night, Three Kings Day, Feast of Jordan, and Old Christmas Day)

January 7
Russian Orthodox Christmas

A pear poached in red wine is a simple yet exquisite treat. Begin with a peeled pear for each serving, cut it in half, and remove the core. Place the pears in a heavy pot that just holds them in a single layer. Open a bottle of light- or medium-bodied red wine, pour yourself a glass, and then pour the rest over the pears. Add enough water to just cover them. Simmer over medium heat until the pears are tender and then transfer them with a slotted spoon to a serving platter. Keep the pears warm or chill them. Add ½ cup sugar to the poaching liquid, turn the heat to high, and reduce the liquid until it is thick and syrupy. Drizzle the syrup over the pears and serve them immediately, accompanied by a glass of red wine.

January 21
International Hot and Spicy Food Day

Thinness is a horrible calamity for women: Beauty to them is more than life itself and it consists above all of the roundness of their forms and the graceful curvings of their outlines. The most artful toilette, the most inspired dressmaker, cannot disguise certain lacks, nor hide certain angles; and it is a common saying that a scrawny woman, no matter how pretty she may look, loses something of her charm . . . for women who are born thin and whose digestion is good, we cannot see why they should be any more difficult to fatten than young hens; and if it takes a little more time than with poultry, it is because human female stomachs are comparatively smaller, and cannot be submitted, as are those devoted barnyard creatures, to the same rigorous and punctually followed diet.

—Jean Anthelme Brillat-Savarin, *The Physiology of Taste*

Brussels sprouts, *high in vitamins A and C as well as several substances believed to fight infections and inhibit cancers, are one of our most maligned vegetables. But cooked properly (rather than nearly to mush, the reason for their poor reputation), they are a delight. Simmer Brussels sprouts briefly—5 to 10 minutes, depending on their size— and drain them. Serve with a drizzle of lemon juice and a spicy aioli.*

January 23
National Pie Day

Butter *may be made from any kind of milk, but the fattest and richest is made from ewe's milk. In every country where I have traveled I have never failed to obtain fresh-churned butter. Wherever I went, I procured cow's, camel's, mare's, or ewe's milk. I filled a bottle with it three quarters full, stoppered it, and fastened it to my horse's neck. My horse did the rest. When I arrived at my destination, I unstoppered the bottle, and there was a piece of butter as large as my fist.*

—Alexander Dumas's *Dictionary of Cuisine*

In the late winter in the Northeast, when the days have grown warm but the nights are still freezing, the sap of the maple tree begins to flow. With snow still on the ground, you can find buckets attached to the trees, collecting the precious liquid that will be boiled down to produce the famous authentic maple syrup, of which there is nowhere near as much as we wish.

February
National Cherry Month

For a change from the ubiquitous cranberry-orange relish, make cranberry soup as part of a festive holiday meal. Simmer a package of cranberries, 3 whole cloves, and a piece of cinnamon with a cup of orange juice, a cup of red wine, a cup of water, and ⅔ cup sugar until the cranberries are soft. Purée and strain or press the mixture through a food mill. Serve hot or chilled, garnished with orange zest and a dollop of crème fraîche.

For a simple, satisfying meal when you are tired from, say, holiday shopping, try this easy recipe. Cook 2 or 3 ounces dried spaghetti for each portion. Drain the spaghetti thoroughly, place it in a large bowl, and toss it with enough full-flavored extra-virgin olive oil to coat it thoroughly. Add ¼ teaspoon ground nutmeg, ¾ teaspoon freshly ground black pepper, and ¼ teaspoon kosher salt per portion, and toss again. Serve immediately with hot bread, a big green salad, and a glass of light-bodied red wine.

Whenever you find yourself with an abundance of fresh **lemons**, preserve them. To make a quart, slice about a dozen small lemons lengthwise into sixths. Toss them with ¾ cup kosher salt and 1 tablespoon sugar, and pack them into a clean quart jar. Add 1 cup fresh lemon juice, cover the jar, and place it in a cool cupboard for 7 days, turning it upside down each morning and righting it at night, so that all the lemons spend time in the liquid. On the seventh day, top off the jar with olive oil. If you will use the lemon slices within a month or so, there is no need to refrigerate them, for that would blunt their flavor. Use preserved lemons as a garnish, or in salads, soups, curries, and rice dishes, or as a simple, tangy snack.

To feel safe and warm on a cold wet night, all you really need is soup.
—Laurie Colwin, *Home Cooking*

Early February

Release of Pliny the Younger by Russian River Brewing Company, available for just two weeks. This triple IPA, which weighs in above 10 percent alcohol, draws legions of passionate fans from all over the United States and beyond, who wait in line, sometimes in driving rain, for as long as 12 hours at this tiny brew pub—it seats just 135 people—in Santa Rosa, California, in the heart of Sonoma Wine Country.

February 11
Cookbook Festival, Fargo, North Dakota

February 28
International Pancake Day

Polenta *is an ideal comfort food, perfect for any meal during the dark days of December and January. The easiest way to make it is to put 1 cup coarse-ground polenta into a 2-quart baking dish, add 4 cups water, 2 teaspoons kosher salt, 2 tablespoons butter cut in pieces, and stir. Set it in a 325 degree oven for 40 minutes. Open the oven, give the polenta a quick stir, and cook an additional 10 minutes. Serve immediately with your favorite topping or sauce: maple syrup for breakfast, Gorgonzola cheese and toasted walnuts for breakfast or dinner, Parmigiano cheese and fresh sage for any meal, simple marinara sauce at any time. The possibilities are limited only by your preferences.*

Last week of February
American Wine Appreciation Week

The Good Cook's Resources

When you stop shopping at a single supermarket for everything that goes into your pantry and onto your table, a world of deliciousness opens up. I always recommend doing your weekly shopping at your local farmers market and then filling in what you need at farm stands and locally owned markets. In Sonoma County, California, where I live, there are six year-round farmers markets and another twenty or so that operate seasonally. I get almost everything I need at these markets, except for a few staples, such as Diamond Crystal Kosher Salt and Tabasco sauce.

When you begin shopping this way, it can be a challenge to remember who has your favorite foods. Where did you get those handmade tortillas? Who has the best prosciutto? Which farmers market does your favorite egg farmer attend? Where can you get harissa, preserved lemons, za'atar, organic whole milk yogurt, wild Gulf shrimp and all the other wonderful foods that you typically cannot find at a supermarket. This section is designed to help you organize this aspect of your life.

Farmers' Markets and Farm Stands

"Eating is a political act, but in the way the ancient Greeks used the word 'political'—not just to mean having to do with voting in an election, but to mean 'of, or pertaining to, all our interactions with other people'—from the family to the school, to the neighborhood, the nation, and the world. Every single choice we make about food matters, at every level. The right choice saves the world."

—Alice Waters

Local Year-Round Farmers Markets

Market _____ Day/Time _____

Location _____ Manager _____

Website & Social Media _____

Favorite Vendors _____

_____

_____

_____

Market _____ Day/Time _____

Location _____ Manager _____

Website & Social Media _____

Favorite Vendors _____

_____

_____

_____

Market _____ Day/Time _____

Location _____ Manager _____

Website & Social Media _____

Favorite Vendors _____

_____

_____

_____

Local Seasonal Farmers Markets

Market _____ Day/Time _____

Season _____

Location _____ Manager _____

Website & Social Media _____

Favorite Vendors _____

_____

_____

_____

Market _____ Day/Time _____

Season _____

Location _____ Manager _____

Website & Social Media _____

Favorite Vendors _____

_____

_____

_____

Market _____ Day/Time _____

Season _____

Location _____ Manager _____

Website & Social Media _____

Favorite Vendors _____

_____

_____

_____

Farm Stands

Name _____ Hours _____

Address _____

Seasons _____ Specialties _____

_____

Name _____ Hours _____

Address _____

Seasons _____ Specialties _____

_____

Name _____ Hours _____

Address _____

Seasons _____ Specialties _____

_____

Name _____ Hours _____

Address _____

Seasons _____ Specialties _____

_____

Name _____ Hours _____

Address _____

Seasons _____ Specialties _____

_____

Name _____ Hours _____

Address _____

Seasons _____ Specialties _____

_____

Community Supported Agriculture

CSA • Subscription Farming • Farm Share • Cow Share

Subscription farming—best known as Community Supported Agriculture, or CSA—began in Japan in the 1960s, spread to western Europe in the early 1970s and then slowly traveled west, first to New England and then to the rest of America. In its purest form, subscribers own a share of the farm for a year; the harvest is divided evenly among them and all share in both abundance and loss. Farmers sell subscriptions based on the number of people their land can feed, plant based on that number—everyone hopes for full enrollment, but not all achieve it—and harvest a bounty of fresh vegetables during the local growing season. If there are crop failures, the impact is spread out so that the farmer does not take the full hit.

Today, most CSA programs operate differently, allowing members to sign up for a month at a time, with discounts for longer subscriptions. Prices range from about $10 a week for what is typically called a "half-share" to about $25 or so, which provides enough produce to feed a family of four. Members pick up their box or basket at the farm or pay a bit more to snag it at a drop-off location or have it delivered to their homes.

Many farms now offer optional add-ons, such as bread, eggs, flowers, fruit, estate preserves and more. With all the options, a subscription can run $60 a week or more, especially if you choose home delivery. Most subscriptions come with a newsletter, featuring stories of the farm, seasonal recipes, and news.

As subscription farming has grown in popularity, ranchers, fishermen and others have launched similar programs. There are cow shares—you buy a portion of the cow and share its milk, popular with people who want raw milk, which is hard to find—and meat CSAs, a few seafood CSAs and even flower CSAs, offering a beautiful locally grown bouquet each week. Many CSAs invite members to the farm, some at almost anytime and others for special celebrations.

These are the purest forms of subscription farming. There are now retail operations that deliver boxes of food each week and call themselves CSAs but these are closer to shopping services, not farm shares. If you want to know your farmer and rancher and be confident in the source of your food, you want the real thing.

A subscription is a wonderful thing to have for yourself but it also makes a wonderful gift, for students heading off to college, for newlyweds, for a dear friend moving to an unfamiliar area.

Community Supported Agriculture

Farm _____ Season _____

Contact Information _____

_____

Frequency _____

Pick Up/Drop Off Location _____

Specialties _____

_____

Add-Ons _____

_____

Cost _____

Special Benefits/Rules _____

_____

Farm _____ Season _____

Contact Information _____

_____

Frequency _____

Pick Up/Drop Off Location _____

Specialties _____

_____

Add-Ons _____

_____

Cost _____

Special Benefits/Rules _____

_____

Farm _____ Season _____

Contact Information _____

_____

Frequency _____

Pick Up/Drop Off Location _____

Specialties _____

_____

Add-Ons _____

_____

Cost _____

Special Benefits/Rules _____

_____

Farm _____ Season _____

Contact Information _____

_____

Frequency _____

Pick Up/Drop Off Location _____

Specialties _____

_____

Add-Ons _____

_____

Cost _____

Special Benefits/Rules _____

_____

Farm _____ Season _____

Contact Information _____

_____

Frequency _____

Pick Up/Drop Off Location _____

Specialties _____

_____

Add-Ons _____

_____

Cost _____

Special Benefits/Rules _____

_____

Farm _____ Season _____

Contact Information _____

_____

Frequency _____

Pick Up/Drop Off Location _____

Specialties _____

Add-Ons _____

_____

Cost _____

Special Benefits/Rules _____

_____

Farm _____ Season _____

Contact Information _____

_____

Frequency _____

Pick Up/Drop Off Location _____

Specialties _____

_____

Add-Ons _____

_____

Cost _____

Special Benefits/Rules _____

_____

Favorite Markets

Favorite Local Supermarket

Name _____ Phone _____

Web Details _____

Address _____

Hours _____ Manager _____

Specialties _____

_____

_____

Favorite Italian/Spanish/European Market

Name _____ Phone _____

Web Details _____

Address _____

Hours _____ Manager _____

Specialties _____

_____

_____

Favorite Middle Eastern/Halal Market

Name _____ Phone _____

Web Details _____

Address _____

Hours _____ Manager _____

Specialties _____

_____

_____

Favorite East Indian Market

Name _____ Phone _____

Web Details _____

Address _____

Hours _____ Manager _____

Specialties _____

_____

_____

Favorite Asian Market

Name _____ Phone _____

Web Details _____

Address _____

Hours _____ Manager _____

Specialties _____

_____

_____

Favorite Latino Market

Name _____ Phone _____

Web Details _____

Address _____

Hours _____ Manager _____

Specialties _____

_____

_____

Favorite Bread Bakery

Name _____ Phone _____

Web Details _____

Address _____

Hours _____ Manager _____

Specialties _____

_____

_____

Favorite Produce Market/Stand

Name _____ Phone _____

Web Details _____

Address _____

Hours _____ Manager _____

Specialties _____

_____

_____

Favorite Butcher

Name _____ Phone _____

Web Details _____

Address _____

Hours _____ Manager _____

Specialties _____

_____

_____

Favorite Seafood Purveyor

Name _____ Phone _____

Web Details _____

Address _____

Hours _____ Manager _____

Specialties _____

_____

_____

Favorite Cheese & Other Dairy

Name _____ Phone _____

Web Details _____

Address _____

Hours _____ Manager _____

Specialties _____

_____

_____

Favorite Deli

Name _____ Phone _____

Web Details _____

Address _____

Hours _____ Manager _____

Specialties _____

_____

_____

Favorite Coffee Purveyor

Name _____ Phone _____

Web Details _____

Address _____

Hours _____ Manager _____

Specialties _____

_____

_____

Favorite Tea Purveyor

Name _____ Phone _____

Web Details _____

Address _____

Hours _____ Manager _____

Specialties _____

_____

_____

Favorite Wine Shop

Name _____ Phone _____

Web Details _____

Address _____

Hours _____ Manager _____

Specialties _____

_____

_____

Other Favorite Markets

Cookware • Housewares • Linens • Flowers • Spices

Name _____ Phone _____

Web Details _____

Address _____

Hours _____ Manager _____

Specialties _____

_____

_____

Name _____ Phone _____

Web Details _____

Address _____

Hours _____ Manager _____

Specialties _____

_____

_____

Name _____ Phone _____

Web Details _____

Address _____

Hours _____ Manager _____

Specialties _____

_____

_____

Name _____ Phone _____

Web Details _____

Address _____

Hours _____ Manager _____

Specialties _____

_____

_____

Name _____ Phone _____

Web Details _____

Address _____

Hours _____ Manager _____

Specialties _____

_____

_____

Name _____ Phone _____

Web Details _____

Address _____

Hours _____ Manager _____

Specialties _____

_____

_____

Name _____ Phone _____

Web Details _____

Address _____

Hours _____ Manager _____

Specialties _____

_____

_____

Favorite Restaurants

I never eat in a restaurant that's over a hundred feet off the ground and won't stand still.

—Calvin Trillin

One cannot think well, love well, sleep well if one has not dined well.

—Virginia Woolf, *A Room of One's Own*

Name _____ Phone _____

Website _____ Twitter _____ Facebook _____

Address _____

Hours _____ Price Range _____

Favorite Dishes _____

_____

Favorite Drinks _____

_____

Name _____ Phone _____

Website _____ Twitter _____ Facebook _____

Address _____

Hours _____ Price Range _____

Favorite Dishes _____

_____

Favorite Drinks _____

_____

Name _____ Phone _____

Website _____ Twitter _____ Facebook _____

Address _____

Hours _____ Price Range _____

Favorite Dishes _____

_____

Favorite Drinks _____

_____

Name _____ Phone _____

Website _____ Twitter _____ Facebook _____

Address _____

Hours _____ Price Range _____

Favorite Dishes _____

_____

Favorite Drinks _____

_____

Name _____ Phone _____

Website _____ Twitter _____ Facebook _____

Address _____

Hours _____ Price Range _____

Favorite Dishes _____

_____

Favorite Drinks _____

_____

Name _____ Phone _____

Website _____ Twitter _____ Facebook _____

Address _____

Hours _____ Price Range _____

Favorite Dishes _____

_____

Favorite Drinks _____

_____

Name _____ Phone _____

Website _____ Twitter _____ Facebook _____

Address _____

Hours _____ Price Range _____

Favorite Dishes _____

_____

Favorite Drinks _____

_____

Name _____ Phone _____

Website _____ Twitter _____ Facebook _____

Address _____

Hours _____ Price Range _____

Favorite Dishes _____

_____

Favorite Drinks _____

_____

Name _____ Phone _____

Website _____ Twitter _____ Facebook _____

Address _____

Hours _____ Price Range _____

Favorite Dishes _____

_____

Favorite Drinks _____

_____

Name _____ Phone _____

Website _____ Twitter _____ Facebook _____

Address _____

Hours _____ Price Range _____

Favorite Dishes _____

_____

Favorite Drinks _____

_____

Name _____ Phone _____

Website _____ Twitter _____ Facebook _____

Address _____

Hours _____ Price Range _____

Favorite Dishes _____

_____

Favorite Drinks _____

_____

Name _____ Phone _____

Website _____ Twitter _____ Facebook _____

Address _____

Hours _____ Price Range _____

Favorite Dishes _____

_____

Favorite Drinks _____

_____

Name _____ Phone _____

Website _____ Twitter _____ Facebook _____

Address _____

Hours _____ Price Range _____

Favorite Dishes _____

_____

Favorite Drinks _____

_____

Name _____ Phone _____

Website _____ Twitter _____ Facebook _____

Address _____

Hours _____ Price Range _____

Favorite Dishes _____

_____

Favorite Drinks _____

_____

Name _____ Phone _____

Website _____ Twitter _____ Facebook _____

Address _____

Hours _____ Price Range _____

Favorite Dishes _____

_____

Favorite Drinks _____

_____

Name _____ Phone _____

Website _____ Twitter _____ Facebook _____

Address _____

Hours _____ Price Range _____

Favorite Dishes _____

_____

Favorite Drinks _____

_____

Name _____ Phone _____

Website _____ Twitter _____ Facebook _____

Address _____

Hours _____ Price Range _____

Favorite Dishes _____

_____

Favorite Drinks _____

_____

Favorites & Where to Find Them

ITEM	BRAND/SOURCE
Bread, Sourdough	
Bread, French	
Bread, Italian	
Bread, specialty	
Cheeses, domestic	
Cheeses, French	
Cheeses, Italian	
Chicken, pastured	
Chicken, smoked	
Farm Eggs, pastured	
Duck, fresh	
Duck, foie gras	
Grass-fed Meats	
Pasta, dry	
Pasta, fresh	
Olive oils	
Butter, from grass-fed cows	
Organic milk, from grass-fed cows	

ITEM	**BRAND/SOURCE**
Specialty Oils (walnut, hazelnut, pumpkin seed)	
Vinegars	
Mustard, Dijon	
Mustard, Brown	
Mustard, Specialty	
Tomatoes, Canned	
Prosciutto, Jamon Serrano	
Pastrami, Corned Beef	
Sausages	
Mexican/Southwestern ingredients	
Southeast Asian ingredients	
Japanese, Chinese, Korean ingredients	

ITEM	BRAND/SOURCE
Gluten-free baked goods	
Gluten-free pastas	
Other favorites	

A Well-Stocked Pantry

With a well-stocked pantry you can rise to nearly any last minute challenge, a stormy night, a cancelled date, or simply the desire to eat well while you hibernate for a few days. These basics will make all your cooking easier and more pleasant.

Salts and Peppers
Flake Salts, Fleur De Sel, Sel Gris, Smoked Salt
Black Peppercorns
White Peppercorns
& herbs & spices

Olive Oils
Pure for cooking,
extra-virgin, good commercial quality
extra-virgin, condiment quality
(Tuscan or Luccese, Provençal, Ligurian, Californian)

Vinegars
Apple Cider, Red Wine (6 to 6.5 acidity)
Champagne (6 to 6.5 acidity), Raspberry (4.5 acidity)
Rice Wine, Sherry, Balsamic

Mustards
Dijon, Coarse Grain, Colman's Dry Mustard Flour, Yellow Mustard Seed

Other Condiments
Soy Sauce, Chutney, Capers, Green Peppercorns, Dried Tomatoes in Olive Oil, Tabasco Sauce, Honey, Sesame Tahini

Dried Goods
Polenta, Stoneground Cornmeal, Cannellini Beans, Black Beans, Pinot Beans, Wild Rice, Arborio Rice, Basmati Rice, Spaghetti, Linguine, Penne, Dried Tomato Bits, Yeast, Bread Flour, Sugar

Canned Goods
Crushed Tomatoes, Whole Tomatoes, Tomato Paste in a Tube, Anchovies, Brisling Sardines, Greek Olives, Green Olives, Tuna, Chickpeas, Chipotle Peppers, Chicken Broth, Coconut Milk

Optimum Storage Times of Common Staples

Olive oils	Cool, dark cupboard, up to 6 months
Olive oil, flavored	Homemade: refrigerator, up to 1 week
	Commercial: cool, dark cupboard, up to 6 months
Walnut oil	Refrigerator, up to 4 months
Hazelnut oil	Refrigerator, up to 4 months
Vinegars	Cool, dark cupboard, up to 2 years
Vinegar, flavored	Cool, dark cupboard, up to 1 year
Mustard, flour	Cool, dark cupboard, up to 1 year
Mustard, prepared	Cool, dark cupboard, up to 3 months; refrigerator, up to 6 months
Soy sauce	Refrigerator, up to 1 year
Dried tomatoes	Cool, dark cupboard, up to 6 months
Dried tomatoes, in oil	Refrigerator, up to 3 months
Polenta	Freezer, up to 6 months
Dried pasta	Cool, dark cupboard, up to 18 months
Rice, most types, including wild	Cool, dark cupboard, indefinitely
Rice, brown	Cool, dark cupboard for 1 month; refrigerator, up to 6 months
Flour, white	Cool, dark cupboard, up to 1 year
Flour, whole wheat	Cool, dark cupboard, 1 month; refrigerator, up to 1 year
Salt, all types	Away from moisture, indefinitely
Yeast	Fresh: refrigerator, up to 2 weeks
	Dry: cool, dark cupboard, until expiration date
Sugar, all types	Indefinitely
Honey	Cool, dark cupboard, up to 1 year
Spices	Ground: cool, dark cupboard, up to 6 months; Whole: 1 year
Tomatoes, canned	Cool, dark cupboard, up to 1 year
Onions	Cool, dark cupboard, up to 3 weeks; never with potatoes, not in plastic

Potatoes	Cool, dark cupboard (45-50°F), up to 2 months; never with onions, not in plastic
Garlic	Cool, dark cupboard, up to 3 months; never in refrigerator, not in plastic
Coffee, whole beans	Refrigerator, 1 month
Tea, loose leaves or bagged	Cool, dark cupboard, up to 1 year
Chocolate	All types: cool, dark cupboard (under 70°F at all times) Dark, up to 1 year; Milk, up to 6 months
Cocoa	Cool, dark cupboard, tightly sealed, up to 1 year
Walnuts	In shell: pantry, 2 to 3 months; refrigerator, up to 1 year; Shelled: refrigerator, up to 1 year
Pine nuts	Refrigerator, up to 1 month
Pecans	In shell: pantry, 2 to 3 months; refrigerator, up to 6 months; Shelled: refrigerator, up to 6 months
Almonds	In shell: pantry, 1 year; Shelled: freezer, up to 3 months

Uses for Vinegar

TYPE OF VINEGAR	PRICE RANGE	RECOMMENDED USES
Balsamic, commercial	Inexpensive to expensive	Sauces, dressings, marinades, condiment
Balsamic, traditional	Extremely expensive	Condiment
Black	Inexpensive	Flavoring, Chinese and other Pacific Rim cuisines
Cane	Inexpensive	Philippine cuisine
Champagne	Moderate	Fruit vinegars, light dressings, soups and stews
Cider	Inexpensive to moderate	Preserves and chutneys, vinaigrettes, shrubs, soups and stews, bone broth, pickling
Distilled (white)	Inexpensive	Cleaning and general household uses
Malt	Inexpensive to moderate	Pickling, ketchup, fish and chips
Pineapple	Moderate	Dressings, salsas, barbecue sauce
Raspberry	Moderate to expensive	Dressings, marinades, emulsions, flavoring, condiment
Red wine	Moderate	Hearty dressings, sauces, marinades, spice vinegars
Rice	Inexpensive to moderate	Southeast Asian and Japanese cuisine, with oysters, seafood
Sherry	Moderate to expensive	Sauces, soups, dressings
White wine	Moderate	Dressings, emulsions, herb vinegars, fruit vinegars

Smoke Points of Recommended Culinary Oils

TYPE OF OIL	SMOKE POINT	SUITABLE COOKING METHODS OR USES
Almond	495°F	Dressings, baking grilled fish
Avocado	520°F	Dressings, frying
Coconut	350°F	sautéing, frying
Grapeseed	446°F	Deep-frying, frying, sautéing
Hazelnut	430°F	Dressings, sauces, flavoring
Macadamia Nut	390°F	Dressings, sautéing
Olive, ultra-premium extra-virgin	250°F	condiment
Olive, extra-virgin	250°F to 420°F	Dressings, flavoring, emulsions, condiment sautéing, frying, deep-frying
Olive, pure refined	410°F	Frying, sautéing, deep-frying
Peanut (ground nut)	450°F	Frying, deep-frying, emulsions, roux
Pumpkin seed	224°F	Dressings, flavoring
Sesame	410°F	Flavoring, stir-frying, sautéing
Walnut	320°F	Dressings, sauces, flavoring, light sautéing

Commercial Mustards

TYPE	CHARACTERISTICS	RECOMMENDED STORAGE	USES
Flour, mild (one of the standard retail dry mustards)	Pale yellow powder, heat on tongue	Pantry, well sealed against dampness	Mild homemade mustard; as a spice; pickling
Flour, hot (one of the standard retail dry mustards)	Deep yellow powder, full vaporizing heat	Pantry, well sealed against dampness	Chinese-style mustard; homemade mustards; as a spice in sauces, dressings; pickling
Colman's Dry	Mix of mild and hot mustard flours	Pantry, well sealed against dampness	English hot mustard; Chinese-style mustard; homemade mustards; as a spice in sauces, dressings; pickling
Seeds, white	Pale yellow seeds	Pantry, well sealed against dampness	Homemade coarse-grain mustard; pickling; Indian spice blends; garnish; sprouts
Seeds, brown	Tiny reddish black seeds	Pantry, well sealed against dampness	Homemade Dijon-style mustard; Indian spice blends; sprouts
American yellow	Sharply acidic but without much heat; made from white mustard seeds only	Refrigeration is not essential, but will help maintain maximum flavor	The basic hot-dog mustard
American brown	Mild with a bit of spiciness, less acidic than American yellow	Refrigeration is not essential, but will help maintain maximum flavor	As a condiment if you prefer a very mild mustard

TYPE	CHARACTERISTICS	RECOMMENDED STORAGE	USES
English hot	Full taste on the tongue and full vaporization; very hot	Refrigeration is not essential, but will help maintain maximum flavor	As a condiment with smoked meats, Cheddar cheese, sausages, roast beef
Dijon	Typical Dijon that has been toned down some	Refrigeration is not essential, but will help maintain maximum flavor	As a condiment; in marinades, sauces, dressings
Dijon, extra-strong, for export	Smooth, suave, French mustard, more pungent than Dijon, but less so than that produced for domestic use in France	Refrigeration is not essential, but will help maintain maximum flavor	As a condiment; in marinades, sauces, dressings
Dijon, extra-forte, French	Smooth, suave, French mustard with full range of pungency	Refrigeration is not essential, but will help maintain maximum flavor	As a condiment; in marinades, sauces, dressings
Bordeaux	Made with whole brown seeds; sweet, spicy, tart	Pantry	As a condiment; on sandwiches, with smoked meats and pates
Meaux	Made with whole brown seeds; slightly spicy, very tart, not sweet	Pantry	As a condiment; on sandwiches, with smoked meats and pates
German hot	Brown, often hot, frequently sweet, and often flavored with horseradish	Refrigeration is not essential, but will help maintain maximum flavor	As a condiment with sausages, smoked meats, pates

TYPE	CHARACTERISTICS	RECOMMENDED STORAGE	USES
Creole	Vary with producer, most often slightly coarse-grained brown mustard, rather tart	Refrigeration may not be essential, but will help maintain flavor; check ingredients list	As a condiment
Dijon-style	Many have an unpleasant floury texture; generally inferior in all ways to French mustards	Refrigeration is not essential, but will help maintain maximum flavor	Limited, unless you find one you particularly like
Flavored Dijon-style	Quality and characteristics vary greatly, as do flavors; those made with true Dijon tend to be best	Refrigeration often essential; check ingredients list	As a condiment
Other flavored mustards	Quality and characteristics vary greatly	Refrigeration often essential; check ingredients list	As a condiment

Tables Of Equivalents

OVEN TEMPERATURES

CASUAL	FAHRENHEIT	CELSIUS	GAS
Very slow	250	121	½
Very slow	275	135	1
Slow	300	148	2
Moderate	325	163	3
Moderate	350	177	4
Moderate	375	190	5
Hot	400	204	6
Hot	425	218	7
Hot	450	232	8
Very hot	475	246	9
Very hot	500	260	10

U.S./U.K.	METRIC
oz = ounce	g = gram
lb = pound	kg = kilogram
in = inch	mm = millimeter
ft = foot	cm = centimeter
tsp = teaspoon	ml = milliliter
tbl = tablespoon	1 = liter
fl oz = fluid ounce	
qt = quart	

LIQUID MEASURES

FLUID OUNCES	U.S. MEASURES	IMPERIAL MEASURE	METRIC
	1 tsp	1 tsp	5 ml
¼	2 tsp	1 dessert spoon	7 ml
½	1 tbl	1 tbl	15 ml
1	2 tbl	2 tbl	28 ml
2	¼ cup	4 tbl	56 ml
4	½ cup (¼ pint)		110 ml
5		¼ pint/1 gill	140 ml
6	¾ cup		170 ml
8	1 cup (½ pint)		225 ml
9			250 ml (¼ liter)
10	1¼ cups	½ pint	280 ml
12	1½ cups (¼ pint)		340 ml
15		¼ pint	420 ml
16	2 cups (1 pint)		450 ml
18	2⅓ cups		500 ml (½ liter)
20	2½cups	1 pint	560 ml
24	3 cups (1½ pints)		675 ml
25		1¼ pints	700 ml
27	3½ cups		750 ml
30	3¾ cups	1½ pints	840 ml
32	4 cups (1 quart)		900 ml
35		1¾ pints	980 ml
36	4½ cups		1000 ml (1 liter)
128	1 gallon (4 quarts, 16 cups)	32 gills	3785 ml (3.75 liters)

SOLID MEASURES

U.S./U.K. OUNCES	U.S./U.K. POUNDS	GRAMS	KILOS
1		28	
2		56	
3½		100	
4	¼	112	
5		140	
6		168	
8	½	225	
9		250	¼
12	¾	340	
16	1	450	
18		500	½
20	1¼	560	
24	1½	675	
27		750	¾
28	1¾	780	
32	2	900	
36	2¼	1000	1

EQUIVALENTS OF COMMON PANTRY STAPLES

WHITE SUGAR

¼ cup	2 oz	60 g
⅓ cup	3 oz	75 g
½ cup	4 oz	125 g
¾ cup	6 oz	185 g
1 cup	8 oz	250 g

BROWN SUGAR

¼ cup	1½ oz	45 g
½ cup	3 oz	90 g
¾ cup	4 oz	125 g
1 cup	5½ oz	170 g
1½ cups	8 oz	250 g

POLENTA/CORNMEAL/LONG-GRAIN RICE

¼ cup	2 oz	60 g
½ cup	2½ oz	75 g
¾ cup	4 oz	125 g
1 cup	5 oz	155 g
1½ cups	8 oz	250 g

DRIED BEANS

¼ cup	1½ oz	45 g
⅓ cup	2 oz	60 g
½ cup	3 oz	90 g
¾ cup	5 oz	155 g
1 cup	6 oz	185 g
1½ cups	8 oz	250 g

ALL PURPOSE FLOUR/DRIED BREAD CRUMBS/CHOPPED NUTS

¼ cup	1 oz	30 g
⅓ cup	1½ oz	45 g
½ cup	2 oz	60 g
¾ cup	3 oz	90 g
1 cup	4 oz	125 g
1½ cups	6 oz	185 g
2 cups	8 oz	250 g

WHOLE-WHEAT FLOUR

3 tbl	1 oz	30 g
½ cup	2 oz	60 g
⅔ cup	3 oz	90 g
1 cup	4 oz	125 g
1¼ cups	5 oz	155 g
1⅔ cups	7 oz	210 g
1¾ cups	8 oz	250 g

HONEY

2 tbl	2 oz	60 g
¼ cup	3 oz	90 g
½ cup	5 oz	155 g
¾ cup	8 oz	250 g
1 cup	11 oz	345 g

GRATED HARD CHEESE (PARMIGIANO/ROMANO/DRY JACK)

¼ cup	1 oz	30 g
½ cup	2 oz	60 g
¾ cup	3 oz	90 g
1 cup	4 oz	125 g
1⅓ cups	5 oz	155 g
2 cups	7 oz	220 g

BUTTER, LARD & DUCK FAT

1 tbl	½ oz	15 g
2 tbl	1 oz	30 g
4 tbl	2 oz	60 g
8 tbl	4 oz	115 g (1 stick, ½ cup)
16 tbl	8 oz	225 g (2 sticks, 1 cup)
32 tbl	16 oz	450 g (4 sticks, 2 cups)

Salts for Your Pantry

Flake Salt

All flake salts are produced similarly, as it takes specific conditions—a heated saturated brine—for salt to form a flake. All flake salts dissolve quickly; for general cooking, price should be a guide.Rice Wine, Sherry, Balsamic

Name	Source, Price	Taste	Best Uses
Cyprus Mediterranean	Cyprus; Seawater; Expensive	Delicate; bright; smooth	Finish
Hana No Shio	Japan; Seawater; Expensive	Delicate; bright; smooth, with snap	Finishing
Kosher (Diamond Crystal brand)	US; Mined; Inexpensive	Smooth, delicate; dry	All purpose cooking, finishing
Maldon	England; Sea water; Moderate	Smooth; delicate; dry	Finishing
Murray River	Australia; Underground salt water deposits; Moderate	Light, delicate, smooth, dry.	Finishing

Solar Dried Salt, Unrefined

The best solar dried sea salts are those that go through no additional processing.

Name	Source, Price	Taste	Best Uses
Celtic Sea Salt (brand name)	Atlantic Coast, France; moderate	Complex; earthy; minerally; moist	Finishing; general cooking
Fleur de Sel	Guerande, France; Seawater; expensive	Delicate; bright; moist	Finishing
Sel gris	Atlantic Coast, France; Seawater; moderate	Complex; earthy; minerally; moist	Finishing; general cooking.
Sel de Guerande	Brittany, France; Seawater; moderate to expensive	Complex; earthy; minerally; moist	Finishing; general cooking

Solar Dried, Refined

Many sea salts—i.e., salt from evaporated sea water—go through additional processing that removes trace minerals and typically creates a small hard cube. These salts may be labeled as sea salt, table salt and, if iodine is added, iodized salt; they often come from the same pile of salt, regardless of their label descriptions. These salts are sometimes called granulated.

Name	Source, Price	Taste	Best Uses
Baleine	Mediterranean coast of France; moderate	Sharp; hard	N/A
Kosher Salt	US	Sharp; hard; so to dissolve	General cooking where flake salt is not available
Sea Salt (sold under many brand names	US; inexpensive	sharp; hard	N/A
Table Salt	World Wide; inexpensive	Sharp; hard	Non-food uses, such as cleaning
Table Salt, Iodized	World Wide, inexpensive	Sharp; hard	General cooking where iodine is not readily available in foods

Mined, Unrefined

All salts may correctly be called sea salt, as all come from sea water, some of it now as ancient inland salt caverns, the most famous of which is currently Himalayan pink salt.

Name	Source, Price	Taste	Best Uses
Himalayan	Pakistan; moderate to expensive	bright; metallic; hard	Finishing; in salt grinders/graters; salt plates, blocks & bowls; rooms made of salt.
Indian Black	India; cheap	strong taste of sulphur, with bass note of salt	Traditional Indian dishes
Utah Red	Utah; inexpensive to moderate	Iron deposits give this salt a taste of blood	Novelty.

Manufactured

This category of salts includes those that have ingredients other than sodium and chloride in the flakes or crystals. The most common is Hawaiian Alaea, which is manufactured to resembled traditional gathered alaea salt, which cannot be sold because it may contain dirt, seaweed and other items. Black salts are typically called "lava salt" because of their color.

Name	Source, Price	Taste	Best Uses
Black Salt	Various; moderate to expesnive	Moderately salty, with a taste of carbon; both flake and rock.	Novelty
Hawaiian Alaea Salt	Various; inexpensive to moderate	Moderately salty; the best have a silky feel on the palate; some taste of iron or blood	Traditional Hawaiian cooking and ceremonies.
Smoked Salt	Various; moderate	Moderately salty, aggressively smoky; the best are flake salts; some are hard	Finishing, especially with eggs and cheese

The Good Cook's Basic Recipes

How To Boil Water • The Simplest Green Salad • Basic Vinaigrette • Perfect Poached Eggs • Farm Egg Omelet • The Best Roasted Chicken • Congee • Slow-Cooker Polenta • Turkey Stock • Strong Stock • Slow-Cooker Bone Broth • Slow-Cooker Chicken Bone Broth • Fish Fumet • The Easiest Dessert • Chai

Somehow I have never minded dining alone. Instead, I find it is a rare opportunity for relaxing and collecting my senses, and I have always made each occasion something of a ceremony. A nicely set table and time—these are as important as the food.

—James Beard

What is the hardest part about getting dinner on the table? It's the thinking about it, the stress of wondering what to cook night after night. Shopping at a farmers market is not only the best thing to do for your community; it is also the best way to solve the dinner dilemma, because the market will tell you what to cook. Simply go, open your eyes, buy some things that look good, return home, cook, eat. Problem solved. Deliciously.

If you find cooking dinner night after night a challenge, you might be putting too much pressure on yourself. Here's my advice. Learn to cook so that you don't need to rely on recipes, especially on weeknights. If you can make a simple green salad, an omelet, a few vegetable dishes, a soup or two, a couple of rice dishes, a few pastas and roast a chicken without opening a cookbook or searching online for a recipe, you're good to go from Monday through Thursday nights for months. Variety comes from the seasonal ingredients you'll naturally snag from the farmers markets; you won't get stuck in a rut because nature won't let you.

If you want to experiment with recipes or new kinds of cuisines, you've got weekends, holidays and vacations for that.

As a culture, we have come to think of cooking as hard because our food-as-entertainment industry tells us it is, not so much directly but in a thousand little ways every day, from Iron Chef–style competitions to nonstop praise for so-called celebrity chefs. But the Thomas-Keller-does-it-better-than-I-ever-could attitude is simply wrong. Never doubt that the best food in the world is cooked at home, everywhere, the world around. If you've ever eaten at the French Laundry or similar restaurants, you understand that you would never want to eat that way day in and day out. Don't believe me? Just ask Anthony Bourdain; he makes this point repeatedly.

True simplicity, based on the seasons and enduring techniques passed down through generations, is its own reward.

The recipes in this section are the ones, if you can commit them to memory—feel free to make them your own, with whatever variations you prefer—will lower your stress and increase your happiness in the kitchen.

How To Boil Water

In the early 1990s, I attended the School for American Chefs at Beringer Vineyards, a sort of graduate seminar for working chefs led by renowned cookbook author Chef Madeleine Kamman.

Madeleine had two assistants, one a young man eager to be helpful. A very touching moment came when the senior assistant, an accomplished young woman, asked him to let her know when a saucepan of water reached a boil.

He stood there, staring at the pan. After several minutes, he confessed, looking meek and shy, that he didn't know how to tell if the water was boiling or not. It was something he simply had never seen before.

It was a revelation.

We are not born knowing how to boil water and if we grow up in a home where no one cooks, how do we learn? It is something everyone should know, not just for cooking but for emergencies, when the water supply is limited or tainted or a baby's a-birthin' unexpectedly.

So, how do you boil water? Put water into a cooking vessel, set it over a high flame or hot burner and wait until large bubbles rise from the bottom of the pot to the surface in a roiling churning frenzy.

This is what is called a rolling boil.

The vessel you choose will depend on what you plan to do once the water boils. If you are making tea, use a tea kettle; if pasta, use a large pot so that the water returns to a boil quickly after the pasta is added, thus preventing the pasta from becoming soggy. In between these two extremes, a closed container for tea and a large pot for pasta, there are myriad choices, which will become intuitive quickly, as you become a good cook.

The Simplest Green Salad

Serves 2, easily increased

Most of us know the term "insalata," Italian for salad. We see it on menus everywhere. But the complete term is un'insalata, which means, literally, that which is salted, which refers to the age-old technique of adding salt to salad greens first, before any other ingredients. By doing so, the flavors blossom quickly and you actually use less salt than if you add it after dressing the salad.

3 or 4 large handfuls of fresh leafy salad greens, clean and dry
Flake salt
Extra-virgin olive oil
Acid of choice (lemon juice, white wine vinegar, red wine vinegar, apple cider vinegar)
Black pepper in a mill

Put the greens into a spacious bowl, sprinkle light with salt and toss. Drizzle with a bit of olive oil, enough to coat the leaves but not pool in the bottom of the bowl. Sprinkle acid over the greens, using about a third as much as you did of the oil. Toss, correct for salt and acid balance, season with pepper and enjoy.

Basic Vinaigrette

Makes about ⅓ cup

There is no good reason to buy commercial salad dressings. They are expensive, you have to recycle the bottle and they are always filled with ingredients you don't really want or understand, emulsifiers, preservatives and flavors that have little if anything to do with the ingredients they attempt to mimic. A vinaigrette takes just a couple of minutes to make and is best used immediately. Use this recipe as a template, varying the flavors based on the type of acid and the type of oil you use. For my deeper exploration of vinaigrettes, other dressings and their broad application take a look at my book Vinaigrettes and Other Dressings *(Harvard Common Press, 2013), which includes recipes for making such classic commercial dressings as Ranch and Blue Cheese at home.*

Do not think of a vinaigrette as just a dressing for salads; vinaigrettes are wonderful on everything from summer tomatoes and fresh mozzarella to roasted chicken, grilled hangar steak, sliced potatoes and so much more.

1 small shallot, minced
Flake salt
1 tablespoon acid (citrus juice, vinegar)
3 to 4 tablespoons extra-virgin olive oil or a combination of extra-virgin olive oil and a
    cold-pressed nut oil (walnut, hazelnut, roasted peanut)
Black pepper in a mill

Put the shallot into a small canning jar, season with a pinch or two of salt and add the acid. Let sit for a few minutes, add the oil, seal the jar and shake. Taste, correct for salt and season with a few turns of black pepper. Use right away.

Perfect Poached Eggs

Poached eggs are delicious in simple green salads and on top of shell beans, simple pastas, and polenta. Serve them neat, with toast, for breakfast but don't forget about them for lunch and dinner, too.

Select the best eggs available, preferably from a farm stand or farmers market.

For 2 eggs, fill a small saucepan about half full with water and add a splash—about a teaspoon, but don't bother measuring—of white wine vinegar. Set the pan over high heat.

Break an egg into a small bowl and when the water reaches a rolling boil, carefully tip the egg into the pan. Working quickly, break the second egg into the bowl and add it, placing it away from the first egg.

Set the timer for 2 minutes and adjust the heat as needed so that the water simmers but does not boil over.

At the end of 2 minutes, look at the eggs and if the whites are still transparent, cook 30 to 60 seconds more. Use a slotted spoon to gently lift the eggs from the water, one at a time, and set on a clean tea towel to drain briefly. Transfer to a plate or bowl, season with salt and pepper and enjoy immediately.

Farm Egg Omelet

Serves 2, easily doubled

Somewhere along the line, America's concept of the omelet went terribly wrong. Instead of eggs, cooked quickly, to be enjoyed for themselves, it became an emnvelop to hold mounds of other ingredients. In many cases, the eggs are more of an afterthought. But if you've ever had an omelet in France—typically at lunch, sometimes at dinner—you'll understand the appeal of a true omelet's simplicity: Good eggs, good butter, a bit of salt and pepper. If you want to add a filling, think equally simply, adding some sautéed mushrooms, perhaps, a bit of Gruyere cheese or sliced avocado. When tomatoes are in season, I typically top an omelet with warm cherry tomato vinaigrette.

4 large farm eggs
Flake salt
Black pepper in a mill
4 teaspoons butter

Break 2 eggs into 2 small bowls, add 2 teaspoons of warm water to both bowls and beat the eggs until smooth, using a fork or small whisk. Season with salt and pepper.

Set a 9-inch omelet pan over high heat, add half the butter and when it is very foamy, tip the pan to coat it carefully with the butter. Working quickly, tip in 2 eggs and let cook, without stirring, for about 90 seconds. Continue to cook while using a fork to whip the unset eggs into tender curds, being certain not to reach down through the set portion.

When the eggs are fully set but still moist, use a spatula to lift the portion of the omelet near the handle and fold it over, leaving about a third of the omelet exposed. Using your non-dominant hand, lift the pan and tip the handle up and over a small plate, so that the omelet drops onto the plate, neatly folded in thirds.

Repeat with the second bowl of eggs.

Serve neat or with whatever condiments you prefer.

The Best Roasted Chicken

Serves 3 to 4

Try to find chicken raised outside close to where you live. I do not recommend caged chicken from a national producer, as those birds live miserable lives, typically retain residual antibiotics and toxins and lack both flavor and muscle tone. The best way to find local chicken is to ask at your local farmers market; if no one has it, chances are good a farmer will know who does.

1 pastured chicken, about 4 to 4½ pounds
Chicken innards, optional
Kosher salt
Black pepper in a mill
2 tablespoons chicken fat, duck fat or butter
2 tablespoons organic butter
3 generous handfuls of fresh herbs, arugula, frisee, watercress or other mixed greens

Preheat the oven to 425 degrees.

Rinse the chicken under cool tap water (in an empty sink) and dry it with a clean tea towel.

Season the cavity of the chicken with salt and pepper. If you have the innards, tuck them into the cavity.

Bend the wing tips back and under the chicken. Use kitchen twine to tie the chicken legs together.

Put the poultry fat or butter into a small saucepan set over low heat.

Place the chicken on a rack set in a roasting pan just big enough to hold it. Season all over with salt and pepper. Use a pastry brush to coat it with fat or butter.

Cook, basting the chicken every 10 minutes or so with the melted fat or butter, for about one hour, or less if the chicken is smaller than 4 pounds.

Remove the chicken from the oven, transfer it to a platter and cover loosely with a tent of aluminum foil.

Set the roasting pan over a medium flame, add a quarter cup of water and swirl and scrape the pan to deglaze it. Tip the juices into a small saucepan and add any juices

148

that have collected on the plate with the chicken. If using the innards, carefully extract them and add to the saucepan, along with any juices in the cavity. Simmer over medium heat until the juices are reduced to about a quarter cup. Use a slotted spoon to remove the innards, add the remaining 2 tablespoons of butter and swirl the pan until it melts. Remove from the heat.

Carve the chicken, cutting the leg-thigh pieces off first and then slice the breast and remove the wings.

Put the greens on a platter, sprinkle with salt and toss gently. Arrange the chicken on top, spoon the sauce over the chicken and serve immediately.

Reserve the carcass and the innards for stock.

Congee

Congee—also called chok, jook, porridge, babaw and a variety of other names—is known throughout much of Asia, where it is eaten as a restorative, a hangover preventative and/or cure, a simple healthy breakfast and a late night snack when heading home from a night on the town. When suffering from a cold or flu, I eat it daily—sometimes for breakfast, lunch and dinner—until my appetite returns. I've also fed it to my pups when they've suffered digestive upset. When convalescing, it is best to use white rice, which is easier to digest. To enjoy at the peak of health, use brown rice if you prefer. If you have a busy week, you can make a double batch on Sundays and the entire family can enjoy it for breakfast all week. Enjoy it neat or with one of the suggested toppings.

¾ cup organic Jasmine rice
2 teaspoons kosher salt
1 tablespoon cold-pressed peanut oil
8 cups homemade chicken stock, chicken-
  mushroom stock or mushroom stock, see
  Note below

Fish sauce, soy sauce, toasted sesame oil,
  lime or lemon wedge, hot sauce of
  choice

Put the rice, salt, peanut oil and stock into a medium saucepan, set over high heat, bring to a boil and immediately reduce the heat so that the mixture simmers very slowly. Simmer until the rice has begun to fall apart, about 2 or even 3 hours. Alternately, prepare the congee in a pressure cooker; it will take about 1½ hours or a tad longer.

Cool a bit, ladle into a cup or bowl and enjoy neat or with condiments and toppings of choice.

NOTE
I tend to prefer a fairly loose congee, closer to soup than, say, creamy polenta. If you prefer a thicker version, increase the rice to 1½ cups or reduce the stock to 5 to 6 cups.

Serving suggestions:

- Top with a poached egg or soft-boiled egg and a shake of hot sauce.
- Top with cooked wild salmon.
- Top with greens sautéed with garlic.
- Top with roasted chicken, a squeeze of lemon or lime juice and some chopped cilantro.
- Top with cooked and shredded pork or Korean-style barbecued ribs.

151

Polenta in a Crock Pot or Slow Cooker

Makes 12 to 16 servings

If you need to feed a large group, you'll love this recipe! You can even double it simply by using two slow cookers. Of the thousands of recipes I've published over the years, this is my second most requested dish (the first is Preserved Lemons). When I serve this in the morning—sometimes I invite students for breakfast before a field trip—I offer several savory and several sweet toppings. When I serve it at dinner, I typically offer just two, one with meat and one for vegetarians.

3 cups polenta, as fresh as possible (see Note below)
1 tablespoon kosher salt, plus more to taste
6 tablespoons butter, preferably organic
8 ounces grated cheese, Vella Dry Jack, Parmigiano-Reggiano or Pecorino-Romano
    or a mixture of these
Black pepper in a mill
Toppings of choice (suggestions follow)

Pour 12 cups of water into a crock pot or slow cooker and set the control to high. Pour in the polenta, whisking to encourage the grains to separate. Add the salt and cover with the lid.

Give the polenta a quick stir every 15 minutes or so until it begins to thicken, which will take about an hour and a half, possibly two. Reduce the heat to low and cook for 4 to 5 hours, stirring now and then if you think of it. When the polenta is tender and creamy, reset the heat to warm and hold for up to 10 hours. If at any point the polenta seems too thick, thin it with a little water.

To serve, reset the heat to low, stir in the butter and cheese, correct for salt and season with several turns of black pepper.

Let guests serve themselves and choose their toppings from the selection you provide.

Savory Winter Toppings:

- crème fraîche, lemon zest, snipped chives or minced Italian parsley
- Fresh goat cheese, such as chabis, pomegranate arils, black pepper
- Italian-style salsa verde
- Winter greens sautéed with garlic; crisp bacon, crumbled
- Wilted spinach with garlic, lemon and olive oil
- Sautéed broccoli with sliced garlic and red pepper flakes
- Grilled or fried sausages, sliced; minced fresh sage
- Steamed clams or steamed mussels in their broth
- Wild or specialty mushrooms sautéed in butter and a splash of Madeira
- Marinara sauce
- Eggs poached in marinara sauce
- Braised short ribs

Sweet Winter Toppings:

- Butter and maple syrup
- Butter and warm honey
- Organic cream and cinnamon sugar
- Applesauce and cinnamon
- Poached, sweetened cranberries and plain whole milk yogurt
- Winter fruit compote
- Fruit chutney
- Crème fraîche and homemade jam
- Apple butter or pear butter
- Sliced pears or apples sautéed in butter

Basic Turkey Stock

Makes about 8 to 10 cups

One of the saddest sights of the winter holiday season is a discarded turkey carcass, tossed without thought into the trash. I now let friends know I will take whatever turkey carcasses they may have. The weekend of Thanksgiving, my house is typically filled with the aromas of turkey stock, which I make in bulk and freeze in two- and four-cup freezer bags. I use it all year to make soup, gumbo, risotto, and bean dishes.

1 cooked turkey carcass, large pieces of meat removed
Neck, giblets, and other leftover turkey parts, including head and feet
2 bay leaves
1 medium sprig (6 to 8 leaves) fresh sage
1 teaspoon whole black peppercorns
Flake salt

Put the turkey carcass, other turkey parts, bay leaves, sage sprig, and peppercorns in a large soup pot with 4 quarts of water, set over high heat, bring to a boil, and reduce the heat to medium low.

Skim off and discard any foam that forms on top and simmer, partially covered, about 6 hours, until the carcass falls apart.

Strain the stock through a fine sieve or a strainer lined with cheesecloth; discard everything but the stock and let it cool to room temperature.

Skim off the fat on the surface of the stock and discard it. There should be 8 to 10 cups of stock; add water if necessary, or simmer over medium heat until reduced to the correct amount.

Taste and correct for salt.

Use immediately, cool and refrigerate for 3 or 4 days, or freeze for up to 6 months.

Strong Stock

Makes about 12 cups

Strong stock is the classic stock in Chinese and many other Asian cuisines and you'll often find an enormous pot of it in commercial kitchens. It is easy to make at home and quite versatile.

2 pounds pork ribs or necks
2 pounds pork butt or shoulder, fat trimmed
    away, in chunks
3 pounds chicken, cut into pieces
¼ cup kosher salt
2 tablespoons peanut oil or olive oil
2 shallots, thinly sliced

1 leek, white part only, thinly sliced
1 bunch green onions, trimmed and
    chopped
1 ham hock
3 ounces fresh ginger, chopped
2 teaspoons white peppercorns

Put the pork and chicken in a large stockpot, add the salt and enough water to cover and let sit for 30 minutes. Meanwhile, heat the oil in a wok or sauté pan set over medium heat. Add the shallots, leeks and scallions and cook, stirring frequently, until limp, about 7 minutes.

Drain the pork and chicken, rinse the pot and return the meats to the pot. Add the cooked vegetables, the ham hock, the ginger, the peppercorns and enough water to cover everything by 2 inches.

Set the pot over high heat and bring to a boil. Skim off any foam that forms on top and reduce the heat to low. Simmer very gently for at least 5 hours, adding water as necessary to keep the ingredients covered. Do not stir; continue to cook until the stock is rich and concentrated.

Remove from the heat, cool and gently pour the stock through a strainer into a large container.

Cover and refrigerate the stock until fully chilled. Remove and discard the fat that congeals on the surface of the stock.

Use within 3 days or freeze and use within 3 months.

About Bone Broth

References to bone broth are everywhere these days, to the extreme annoyance of many food professionals, from chefs to writers. "It's just stock!" they shout, rolling their eyes at yet another fad. I'll take no small amount of heat from my peers for addressing it here.

But I think it's a good thing. For a long time, home cooks have been afraid of making stock, tending to think of it as a mystery ingredient that belongs in professional not home kitchens. If calling it bone broth instead of stock dissolves the mystery and makes home cooks less leery of it, I'm all for it.

It wasn't always this way. For centuries human wisdom has relied upon slow-cooked bones as a restorative and as a basic ingredient. It has long been given to new mothers, ailing children, cancer patients and others in need of a boost. When I'm feeling poorly, I enjoy a cup of hot bone broth with a squeeze of lemon, a clove of garlic and freshly ground black pepper. During a lengthy illness—I'm prone to getting bad flus—I'll keep a slow-cooker of bone broth going for several days.

One reason for the revival of bone broth is the increasing availability of grass-fed meats and pastured chickens and a deepening understanding of true sustainability. Using all parts of an animal whose life has been sacrificed that we may eat is the best way to honor it. If we eat meat, it makes sense to include the bones in our diet and the way to do this is by making bone broth.

What's the difference between stock and broth? Both exist on the same continuum and their definitions are not set in stone. In general, broth has a greater percentage of flesh, stock a higher proportion of bone, though exact proportions are not crucial. Bone broth also has a generous splash of vinegar, typically organic apple cider vinegar, to facilitate the extraction of calcium and trace minerals.

Slow-Cooker Bone Broth

Makes about 8 to 10 cups

Making bone broth, either on top of the stove or in a slow cooker, is an imprecise technique.

I do not worry about measuring any of the ingredients, though I am careful not to add more than 2 tablespoons of vinegar, lest it influence the taste rather than simply assist with the extraction of minerals, its intended purpose. It is something every generation of home cooks has known how to do, until the last generation or so. The technique should be revived and passed on to our younger family members. Once done, the broth can be seasoned simply, with salt and pepper, and enjoyed as it is or it can be used in other recipes.

5 to 6 pounds meaty bones (a single type or a mix of beef, lamb, goat or pork)
Kosher salt
Filtered or spring water, hot
2 tablespoons apple cider vinegar
1 carrot, in chunks, optional
1 yellow onion, quartered, optional
3 shallots, halved, optional
3 to 4 garlic cloves, optional
1 or 2 parsley sprigs, optional

Preheat the oven to 350 degrees.

Put the bones on a baking sheet or in a roasting pan and season all over with kosher salt. Set in the oven and roast until evenly browned, about 20 to 25 minutes.

Transfer the bones to a slow cooker and add the hot filtered or spring water, covering the bones by 1 or 2 inches. Add 2 tablespoons of the apple cider vinegar and whatever optional ingredients you want. Cook on high for 1 hour and then program on low for 12 hours or as long as your slow cooker will allow.

Cook the bones for a total of 24 hours.

Check the liquid now and then, adding more as needed to keep the bones submerged. Skim off and discard the foam and other impurities that rise to the surface.

After 12 hours, you can remove a ladle or two to use immediately and replace it with fresh water. Use more broth as needed, always replacing it with fresh water.

After 24 hours, gently pour the broth into a container and cover the bones with fresh water and add the remaining 2 tablespoons of vinegar. Cook the second batch for 48 to 72 hours.

Cool the first batch of broth to room temperature, cover it and refrigerate until thoroughly chilled; overnight is best. Remove and discard the layer of fat that has congealed on the surface of the broth. Transfer to another container, leaving behind the layer of impurities at the bottom of the stock.

As the second batch of broth cooks, use it for cooking dried beans and in soups that do not need a stronger broth; always top off with water. When the flavors diminish completely or to where you no longer like them, discard the bones and other ingredients.

Use remaining broth within 3 or 4 days or freeze for up to 3 months.

Slow-Cooker Chicken Bone Broth

Makes 6 to 8 cups

You can, of course, use the bones of a roasted chicken to make this broth. But if you're setting out to make chicken bone broth, this is the technique I recommend.

1 whole pastured chicken, preferably a heritage meat breed
Kosher salt
1 small carrot, in chunks
2 shallots, halved, or 1 yellow onion, quartered
3 or 4 garlic cloves
2 or 3 parsley sprigs
1 slice of fresh ginger, optional
1 teaspoon white peppercorns, optional
Filtered or spring water
2 tablespoon apple cider vinegar

Rinse the chicken in cool running water and put it in a large saucepan or stock pot. Season well with salt. Add the carrot, shallots or onion, garlic, parsley and the ginger and peppercorns, if using. Cover with filtered water by 2 inches and bring to a boil over medium-high heat. The moment the water begins to boil, cover the pan and turn off the heat. Let sit for 1 hour.

Uncover the pot and use tongs or a carving fork to transfer the chicken to a platter to cool. When it is cool enough to handle, remove the meat from the chicken and refrigerate it, covered, until ready to use.

Put the chicken carcass and other bones into a slow cooker, strain the poaching liquid into the cooker and add more water as needed to cover the bones. Add the vinegar and cook on low for12 to 18 hours, using the broth as you like and always topping off with water. Skim off any foam or other impurities that rise to the surface.

Strain the broth into a clean container, cool, refrigerate and then remove the layer of fat that congeals on the top of the broth.

Use the broth within 3 to 4 days or freeze for up to 3 months.

Fish Fumet

Makes 4 to 6 cups

Many home cooks balk at the thought of making fish stock, correctly called fish fumet. But it seems much more daunting than it actually is and it provides wonderful flavor and texture to certain dishes, such as paella. The secret to making a good fish fumet is quite simple. First, do not use an oily fish, such as salmon or mackerel, and, second, do not overcook it lest strong fishy flavors develop. If you want to concentrate the fumet, do so after you've strained it, not before. Use the fumet for soup, stew, risotto, paella and the Catalan pasta dish known as fideua, which, at its best, is short pasta strands (1-inch maximum) toasted until deeply colored and cooked, as risotto is cooked, in fish fumet and served topped with a generous dollop of aioli.

3 pounds fish frames and heads, rinsed in cool water
1 yellow onion, quartered
3 sprigs Italian parsley
1 bay leaf
½ lemon
1 cup dry wine
1 teaspoon black peppercorns
Flake salt

Put all of the ingredients into a soup pot, cover with 4 to 6 cups of water and bring to a boil over high heat. Reduce the heat, skim off any foam that collects on top of the liquid and simmer very gently for 30 minutes. Remove from the heat, cool slightly and strain into a clean container. Season to taste with salt.

Cool completely and store in the refrigerator for up to 3 days and in the freezer for up to 3 months.

The Easiest Dessert

I've always felt the main function of dessert is to give you something to do while you continue your dinner table conversation. It's not about tucking into a mound of chocolate or a rich pie, at least not every night. A few segments of a sweet tangerine or tangy-sweet grapefruit will refresh you and nourish you. As the year progresses, you can do the same thing with strawberries, cherries, apricots, peaches, nectarines, figs, and melons, all in their own season.

4 honey tangerines, 4 oranges, 2 Ruby grapefruit or 1 pomelo

As you and your friends and family chat, pick up a tangerine, orange, grapefruit or pomelo and peel it. Break it into segments and pass them around. Peel another as you continue to chat.

Chai

Makes 8 cups

Of all the foods that have become available in shelf-stable containers on supermarket shelves, the one that has most puzzled me is chai. I'm always astonished to see it and even more surprised when I hear people wonder what is in it. "Chai" is simply the Indian term for tea and refers to black tea, with milk, sugar and a few spices. It is always better, cheaper and more nutritious when you make it at home. And it is so easy to do so. If you really love it, use this recipe to make a batch that will last two or three days. Simply reheat it, cup by cup, as you like.

1 quart whole milk
1 quart water
⅓ cup sugar, plus more to taste
2½ tablespoons Darjeeling tea leaves
2 slices fresh ginger, gently crushed
1 3-inch stick cinnamon
1 teaspoon black peppercorns
2 cloves
2 green cardamom pods, crushed open
Several gratings from whole nutmeg

Bring the milk, water, sugar, and tea to a boil in a heavy saucepan. Remove the pan from the heat, add the spices, cover, and let steep for 15 minutes. Return to high heat, and, just before it boils, strain the chai into a teapot or individual teacups and serve immediately. To store: strain, let it cool, and store it in the refrigerator, covered, for 3 to 4 days. (I find quart canning jars are perfect for storing chai.)

Reheat before serving.

How To Cook Rice & Grains

"Rice is magical. Rice is an explanation of everything."
—Anthony Bourdain, smithsonian.com, July 2014

To serve a simple rice or grain accompaniment, follow these basic guidelines. In all cases, add a teaspoon of salt to the cooking water. In addition, other liquids such as stock or part stock and part water may be used. Consult specific recipes for such changes. Unless otherwise indicated, all grains should cook at a light simmer over low to medium-low heat.

GRAIN PORTION	QUANTITY	LIQUID	COOKING TIME	YIELD/PORTION
Rice, long grain	1 cup	1⅔ cup cold water	20 minutes, tightly covered, low heat; let rest 10 minutes after cooking	3 cups/ 6 servings
Rice, Basmati	1 cup, rinsed	2 cups cold water	20 minutes, tightly covered, low heat; let rest 10 minutes after cooking	3 cups/ 6 servings
Rice, brown	1 cup	2½ cups boiling water	40 to 50 minutes, covered	3 to 4 cups/ 6 to 8 servings
Rice, wild	1 cup, rinsed	4 cups cold water	45 minutes, covered	3½ to 4 cups/ 6 to 8 servings
Polenta, stove top	1 cup	4 cups cold water	20–40 minutes, uncovered; stir frequently	3½ to 4 cups/ 4 to 6 servings
Polenta, double boiler	1 cup	4 cups boiling water	1½ hours, covered, in a double boiler over low heat; stir occasionally	3½ to 4 cups/ 4 to 6 servings
Polenta, oven	1 cup	4 cups boiling water, plus 2 tablespoons butter	Bake at 350°F for 40 minutes, stir, bake additional 10 minutes	3½ to 4 cups/ 4 to 6 servings
Hominy Grits	1 cup	4 cups boiling water	30 minutes, uncovered, stir occasionally	3½ to 4 cups/ 4 to 6 servings
Farro	1 cup	4 cups boiling water	40 to 50 minutes, covered	3½ to 4 cups/ 4 to 6 servings

GRAIN PORTION	QUANTITY	LIQUID	COOKING TIME	YIELD/PORTION
Barley	1 cup, soaked overnight in water	4 cups boiling water	40 to 50 minutes, covered	3½ to 4 cups/ 4 to 6 servings
Quinoa	1 cup, rinsed	2 cups cold water	15 minutes, covered, plus 10 minutes resting off heat	3 cups/ 4 to 6 servings

The Good Cook's Sources

A not-quite-random list of festivals, purveyors of good things to eat and drink and good information about things that interest me and may interest, you, too.

ART OF EATING, THE
P. Box 333, St. Johnsbury, Vermont 05819,
artofeating.com
Edward Bear's highly regarded culinary periodical.

BANDON CHAMBER OF COMMERCE
300 Second St., Bandon, OR 97411, (503)
347-9616, bandon.com
Information on the Bandon Cranberry Festival, held early each fall.

BAT CONSERVATION INTERNATIONAL
P. O. Box 162603 Austin, TX 78716-2603
(512) 327-9721, batcon.org
Everything you might want to know about bats, bat houses, and more, with a beautiful newsletter for members.

BELZONI-HUMPHREYS COUNTY DEVELOPMENT FOUNDATION, INC.
P. O. Box 145, Belzoni, MS (601) 247-4238
Information about the World Catfish Festival.

BEN KINMONT BOOKSELLER
P6780 Depot St., Suite 150, Sebastopol, CA
(707)829-8715, kinmont.com
Antiquarian books, with a focus on food and wine, domestic and rural economy, health, perfume and the history of taste between the 15th and 19th centuries

BLAND FARMS
P. O. Box 506 Glennville, GA 30427 (800)
VIDALIA, blandfarms.com

One of the largest growers and shippers of Vidalia onions. Catalog.

CASTROVILLE ARTICHOKE FESTIVAL
10700 Merritt St., Castroville, CA 95012
((831) 633-2465, artichoke-festival.org
Information about the festival.

CHIPPOKES PLANTATION STATE PARK
P. O. Box 116, Surry, VA 23883,
porkpeanutpinefestival.org 5
Information regarding the Pork, Peanut, and Pine Festival.

CORTI BROTHERS
5810 Folsom Boulevard Sacramento, CA 95819
(916) 736-3800, cortibrothers.com
Excellent array of extra-virgin olive oils, authentic balsamic vinegars, specialty salt, wine and many other products; will ship.

CRANBERRY INSTITUTE
P. O. Box 497, Carver, MA 02330,
(508)866-1118, cranberryinstitute.org
All manner of information on cranberries. Newsletter for members.

D'ARTAGNAN, INC.
280 Wilson Ave., NJ 07105 (800) 327-8246
Excellent source for foie gras, charcuterie, truffles, mushrooms, game birds and game. Catalog.

DAVERO
766 Westside Road Healdsburg, CA 95448,
(707) 431-8000, davero.com
Producers of ultra-premium estate olive oil, Italian varietal wines and more. Tasting room open daily. Mail oder.

G & R FARMS
Route 3, Box 35A Glennville, GA 30427 (800) 522-0567
Vidalia onion farmers since 1945. Catalog; mail order.

RATTO INTERNATIONAL MARKET & DELI
821 Washington Street Oakland, CA 94607 (510) 832-6503, rattos.com
Excellent source for grains, beans, flours, vinegars, olive oils, French butter, spices, and more. Will ship.

GILROY GARLIC FESTIVAL
P. O. Box 2311 Gilroy, CA 95020 (408) 842-1625
Information on the largest of the country's garlic festivals.

GUMBO FESTIVAL
P. O. Box 7069 Bridge City, LA 70094
Information on the festival.

HEIRLOOM TOMATO FESTIVAL, KENDALL-JACKSON VINEYARD ESTATES
5007 Fulton Rd., Fulton, CA 95439, kj.com (707)433-6000
A celebration and tasting of the year's tomatoes, with more than 150 estate-grown varieties, chef competitions, wine pairings and more.

INTERNATIONAL BANANA FESTIVAL
Fulton, KY, (270) 472-9000, thebananafestival.net
Information about the annual festival.

KERMIT LYNCH WINE MERCHANT
1605 San Pablo Avenue Berkeley, CA 94702-1317 (510) 524-1524, kermitlynch.com
Excellent source for French and Italian wines, plus a limited but choice selection of food products, including the best Dijon mustard, anchovies in olive oil, olives, tapenade, lavender honey, and extra-virgin olive oils from Provence, Tuscany, and Liguria. Newsletter, too.

KING ARTHUR FLOUR
The Bakers Catalogue Route 2, Box 56 Norwich, VT 05055 (800) 827-6836
Grains, flours, other ingredients, and equipment for the home baker.

KITCHEN ARTS & LETTERS
1435 Lexington Avenue New York, NY 10128 (212) 876-5550, kitchenartsandletters.com
A bookstore devoted exclusively to food and wine. Mail and phone orders.

LOCAL SPICERY
80-F Main St., Tiberon, CA 94920, (415)435-1100, localspicery.com
Purveyors of freshly milled spices, whole spices, including peppercorns, signature blends, salts and more, including a spice-of-the-month club. A retail location opens in late spring, 2015.

MARION COUNTY CHAMBER OF COMMERCE
1239 North Spalding Ave., Suite 201, Lebanon, KY 40033 (270) 692-9594, lebanon-ky.com
Information regarding Ham Days.

THE MEADOW

523 Hudson St., New York City, 10014, (212) 645-4633, atthemeadow.com
Purveyors of over 100 specialty salts, salt blocks and bowls and more, with three locations, two in Portland, Oregon, and this one. Home of America's first selmelier, Mark Bitterman

NAPA VALLEY MUSTARD FESTIVAL

P. O. Box 3603 Yountville, CA 94599 (707) 938-1133, mustardfestival.org
Information on a month's worth of events.

NATIONAL MUSTARD MUSEUM

7477 Hubbard Ave., Middleton, WI 53562, (800)438-6878, mustardmuseum.com
Food emporium with a display collection of nearly 6000 mustards. Hundreds for sale, along with mustard paraphernalia, T-shirts, books, and a newsletter. Newsletter.

NORTH AMERICAN TRUFFLING SOCIETY

P. O. Box 296 Corvallis, OR 97339, natruffling. org
Organization of truffle aficionados.

OCCIDENTAL ARTS & ECOLOGY CENTER

15290 Coleman Valley Rd., Occidental, CA 95465, (707)874-1557, oaec.org
This 80-acre nonprofit center in western Sonoma County hosts classes and workshops, supports an intentional community, maintains the spectacular Mother Garden and hosts what may be the best plant sales on the planet each spring and fall, all with the goal of creating and support ecological literary. Excellent seed saving program.

OLDWAYS

266 Beacon Street, Boston, CA 02116, (617) 421-5500, oldwayspt.org
Education organization that studies traditional diets of various cultures and sponsors research and conferences on various culinary topics. Developed the Mediterranean Diet pyramid.

PARIS-HENRY COUNTY JAYCEES

P. O. Box 444 Paris, TN 38242, worldsbiggestfishfry.com
Information about the World's Biggest Fish Fry.

PEPPER-PASSION

1111 East Madison St., #124, Seattle, WA 98122, (877) 658-3373, pepper-passion.com
Purveyors of peppercorns from a wide selection of producers, including Penja Black, a lovely pepper from Cameroon, Africa, and a small line of pepper grinders, including hand-carved and signed specialty mills of African olive wood.

POCHE'S MEATMARKET AND RESTAURANT

3015 Main Highway, #A, Breaux Bridge, LA 70517 (337) 332-2108, poches.com
Mail-order source for authentic Cajun meats, including cracklins, boudin, and churice (chaurice), a hard-to-find sausage.

POWELL'S BOOKS FOR HOME AND GARDEN

3747 SE Hawthorne Blvd., Portland, OR 97214 (800) 878-7323, powells.com
Excellent collection, including some antiquarian volumes. Mail order.

SALT INSTITUTE
Fairfax Plaza, Suite 600 700 North Fairfax
Alexandria, VA 22314-2040 (703) 549-4648
Consumer information on salt.

SEED SAVERS EXCHANGE
3094 North Winn Road, Decorah, IA 52101
(563) 382-5990, seedsavers.org
*Genetic preservation program, Members exchange
seeds for a small fee; annual yearbook lists all
available varieties.*

SLOWFOOD USA
1000 Dean St., Suite 222, Brooklyn, NY
11238, slowfoodusa.org
*Global organization dedicated to the preservation
of heritage foods, customs and cuisines.*

SONOMA COUNTY WINE LIBRARY
139 Piper St., Healdsburg, CA 95448
(707)433-3772, sonomalibrary.org
*A comprehensive collection of wine information
from around the world, with historical archives,
more than 1000 rare books and more*

TABASCO COUNTRY STORE
Mcllhenny Company Avery Island, LA 70513
(800) 634-9599, tabasco.com

*The first of all Louisiana hot sauce companies offers
a mail-order catalog with the company's classics
as well as an assortment of products not available
elsewhere.*

**TOMATO GENETICS RESOURCE
CENTER**
Genetic Resources Conservation Program
University of California Davis, CA 95616 (916)
757-8920, tgrc.ucdavis.edu
*Major international repository for tomato germ
plasm; collection includes over 3,000 varieties,
with about 1,000 from wild stock.*

VIDALIA ONION FESTIVAL
Vidalia, GA (912)538-8687,
vidaliaonionfestival.com.
Information on the annual festival.

WESTON A. PRICE FOUNDATION
PMB 106-308, 4200 Wisconsin Avenue, NW,
Washington, DC 20016, wastonaprice.org
*Nonprofit educational organization founded on
the nutritional principles of Dr. Weston Price.
Serves as a clearing house of sorts on a wealth of
information, including the dangers of soy, the
benefits of butter, eggs and meats from grass-fed
animals and more.*

Tasting Notes

Cheeses

United States • Ireland • England • France • Italy • Spain • Mexico • Greece • Argentina • Poland • Denmark • Netherlands • Belgium

Name _____ Producer _____

Origin _____ Purchased at _____ Cost _____

Appearance _____ Aroma _____ Texture _____

Taste _____ Finish _____

Best Uses _____

Beverage Pairings _____

Notes _____

_____

_____

Name _____ Producer _____

Origin _____ Purchased at _____ Cost _____

Appearance _____ Aroma _____ Texture _____

Taste _____ Finish _____

Best Uses _____

Beverage Pairings _____

Notes _____

_____

_____

Name _____ Producer _____

Origin _____ Purchased at _____ Cost _____

Appearance _____ Aroma _____ Texture _____

Taste _____ Finish _____

Best Uses _____

Beverage Pairings _____

Notes _____

_____

_____

Name _____ Producer _____

Origin _____ Purchased at _____ Cost _____

Appearance _____ Aroma _____ Texture _____

Taste _____ Finish _____

Best Uses _____

Beverage Pairings _____

Notes _____

_____

_____

Name _____ Producer _____

Origin _____ Purchased at _____ Cost _____

Appearance _____ Aroma _____ Texture _____

Taste _____ Finish _____

Best Uses _____

Beverage Pairings _____

Notes _____

_____

_____

Name _____ Producer _____

Origin _____ Purchased at _____ Cost _____

Appearance _____ Aroma _____ Texture _____

Taste _____ Finish _____

Best Uses _____

Beverage Pairings _____

Notes _____

_____

_____

Name _____ Producer _____

Origin _____ Purchased at _____ Cost _____

Appearance _____ Aroma _____ Texture _____

Taste _____ Finish _____

Best Uses _____

Beverage Pairings _____

Notes _____

_____

_____

Name _____ Producer _____

Origin _____ Purchased at _____ Cost _____

Appearance _____ Aroma _____ Texture _____

Taste _____ Finish _____

Best Uses _____

Beverage Pairings _____

Notes _____

_____

_____

Name _____ Producer _____

Origin _____ Purchased at _____ Cost _____

Appearance _____ Aroma _____ Texture _____

Taste _____ Finish _____

Best Uses _____

Beverage Pairings _____

Notes _____

_____

_____

Name _____ Producer _____

Origin _____ Purchased at _____ Cost _____

Appearance _____ Aroma _____ Texture _____

Taste _____ Finish _____

Best Uses _____

Beverage Pairings _____

Notes _____

_____

_____

Name _____ Producer _____

Origin _____ Purchased at _____ Cost _____

Appearance _____ Aroma _____ Texture _____

Taste _____ Finish _____

Best Uses _____

Beverage Pairings _____

Notes _____

_____

_____

Name _____ Producer _____

Origin _____ Purchased at _____ Cost _____

Appearance _____ Aroma _____ Texture _____

Taste _____ Finish _____

Best Uses _____

Beverage Pairings _____

Notes _____

_____

_____

Name ———————————————— Producer ————————————————

Origin ——————————— Purchased at ——————— Cost ————

Appearance ——————— Aroma ——————— Texture ———————

Taste ———————————————— Finish ———————————

Best Uses ———————————————————————

Beverage Pairings ————————————————————

Notes ————————————————————————

————————————————————————————————

————————————————————————————————

Name ———————————————— Producer ————————————————

Origin ——————————— Purchased at ——————— Cost ————

Appearance ——————— Aroma ——————— Texture ———————

Taste ———————————————— Finish ———————————

Best Uses ———————————————————————

Beverage Pairings ————————————————————

Notes ————————————————————————

————————————————————————————————

————————————————————————————————

Name ———————————————— Producer ————————————————

Origin ——————————— Purchased at ——————— Cost ————

Appearance ——————— Aroma ——————— Texture ———————

Taste ———————————————— Finish ———————————

Best Uses _____

Beverage Pairings _____

Notes _____

_____

_____

Name _____ Producer _____

Origin _____ Purchased at _____ Cost _____

Appearance _____ Aroma _____ Texture _____

Taste _____ Finish _____

Best Uses _____

Beverage Pairings _____

Notes _____

_____

_____

Name _____ Producer _____

Origin _____ Purchased at _____ Cost _____

Appearance _____ Aroma _____ Texture _____

Taste _____ Finish _____

Best Uses _____

Beverage Pairings _____

Notes _____

_____

_____

Name _____ Producer _____

Origin _____ Purchased at _____ Cost _____

Appearance _____ Aroma _____ Texture _____

Taste _____ Finish _____

Best Uses _____

Beverage Pairings _____

Notes _____

_____

_____

Name _____ Producer _____

Origin _____ Purchased at _____ Cost _____

Appearance _____ Aroma _____ Texture _____

Taste _____ Finish _____

Best Uses _____

Beverage Pairings _____

Notes _____

_____

_____

Mustards

Dijon • Brown • Coarse-Grain • English • Hot • Sweet • German • Flavored

Brand _____ Type _____ Country _____

Purveyor _____ Price_____

Color/Appearance _____ Aroma _____

Taste _____

Texture_____ Consistency_____ Acidity_____

Balance _____ Finish _____

Notes _____

_____

Overall Opinion _____ Will Purchase Again _____

Brand _____ Type _____ Country _____

Purveyor _____ Price_____

Color/Appearance _____ Aroma _____

Taste _____

Texture_____ Consistency_____ Acidity_____

Balance _____ Finish _____

Notes _____

_____

Overall Opinion _____ Will Purchase Again _____

Brand _____ Type _____ Country _____

Purveyor _____ Price_____

Color/Appearance _____ Aroma _____

Taste _____

Texture_____Consistency_____Acidity_____

Balance_____ Finish _____

Notes _____

_____

Overall Opinion _____ Will Purchase Again _____

Brand_____ Type _____ Country_____

Purveyor _____ Price_____

Color/Appearance _____ Aroma _____

Taste _____

Texture_____Consistency_____Acidity_____

Balance_____ Finish _____

Notes _____

_____

Overall Opinion _____ Will Purchase Again _____

Extra-Virgin Olive Oil

California • Italy • Sicily • Spain • France • Greece • Tunisia • Chile • Israel

Professional olive oil tasters undergo extensive training and study international guidelines that determine what olive oils can legally use the "extra-virgin" designation. Much of this tasting has to do with detecting defects; certification declares, in part, that the oil is defect-free. The oils must also meet certain chemical guidelines. Casual tasters explore for different reasons, to educate their palates and to find pleasing oils. The best olive oils change from year to year, as they are an expression of their environment, of the land itself, the changing weather, the light and even the temperament of the producer.

Producer_____Country_____Region_____

Date of Production _____ Purveyor _____ Price _____

Varieties of Olives _____

_____

Color & Appearance_____

Taste _____

Texture/Consistency _____ Balance _____ Finish _____

Notes _____

_____

Overall Opinion _____ Will Purchase Again _____

Producer_____Country_____Region_____

Date of Production _____ Purveyor _____ Price _____

Varieties of Olives _____

_____

Color & Appearance_____

Taste _____

Texture/Consistency _____ Balance _____ Finish _____

Notes _____

_____

Overall Opinion _____ Will Purchase Again _____

Producer_____Country_____Region_____

Date of Production _____ Purveyor _____ Price _____

Varieties of Olives _____

_____

Color & Appearance_____

Taste _____

Texture/Consistency _____ Balance _____ Finish _____

Notes _____

_____

Overall Opinion _____ Will Purchase Again _____

The Good Cook's Archives

I feel now that gastronomical perfection can be reached in these combinations: one person dining alone, usually upon a couch or a hill side; two people, of no matter what sex or age, dining in a good restaurant; six people, of no matter what sex or age, dining in a good home.
—M. F. K. Fisher, *An Alphabet for Gourmets*

Memorable Meals

Date _____ Occasion _____ Location _____

Companions _____

_____

Menu _____

_____

_____

Beverages _____

Thoughts _____

_____

_____

Date _____ Occasion _____ Location _____

Companions _____

_____

Menu _____

_____

_____

Beverages _____

Thoughts _____

_____

_____

Date _____ Occasion _____ Location _____

Companions _____

_____

Menu _____

_____

_____

Beverages _____

Thoughts _____

_____

_____

Date _____ Occasion _____ Location _____

Companions _____

_____

Menu _____

_____

_____

Beverages _____

Thoughts _____

_____

_____

Date _____ Occasion _____ Location _____

Companions _____

_____

Menu _____

_____

_____

Beverages _____

Thoughts _____

_____

_____

Date _____ Occasion _____ Location _____

Companions _____

_____

Menu _____

_____

_____

Beverages _____

Thoughts _____

_____

_____

Date _____ Occasion _____ Location _____

Companions _____

_____

Menu _____

_____

_____

Beverages _____

Thoughts _____

_____

_____

Date _____ Occasion _____ Location _____

Companions _____

_____

Menu _____

_____

_____

Beverages _____

Thoughts _____

_____

_____

Date _____ Occasion _____ Location _____

Companions _____

_____

Menu _____

_____

_____

Beverages _____

Thoughts _____

_____

_____

Date _____ Occasion _____ Location _____

Companions _____

_____

Menu _____

_____

_____

Beverages _____

Thoughts _____

_____

_____

Date _____ Occasion _____ Location _____

Companions _____

_____

Menu _____

_____

_____

Beverages _____

Thoughts _____

_____

_____

Date _____ Occasion _____ Location _____

Companions _____

_____

Menu _____

_____

_____

Beverages _____

Thoughts _____

_____

_____

Date _____ Occasion _____ Location _____

Companions _____

_____

Menu _____

_____

_____

Beverages _____

Thoughts _____

_____

_____

Date _____ Occasion _____ Location _____

Companions _____

_____

Menu _____

_____

_____

Beverages _____

Thoughts _____

_____

_____

Date _____ Occasion _____ Location _____

Companions _____

_____

Menu _____

_____

_____

Beverages _____

Thoughts _____

_____

_____

Date _____ Occasion _____ Location _____

Companions _____

_____

Menu _____

_____

_____

Beverages _____

Thoughts _____

_____

_____

Date _____ Occasion _____ Location _____

Companions _____

_____

Menu _____

_____

_____

Beverages _____

Thoughts _____

_____

_____

Date _____ Occasion _____ Location _____

Companions _____

_____

Menu _____

_____

_____

Beverages _____

Thoughts _____

_____

_____

Date _____ Occasion _____ Location _____

Companions _____

_____

Menu _____

_____

_____

Beverages _____

Thoughts _____

_____

_____

Date _____ Occasion _____ Location _____

Companions _____

_____

Menu _____

_____

_____

Beverages _____

Thoughts _____

_____

_____

Date _____ Occasion _____ Location _____

Companions _____

_____

Menu _____

_____

_____

Beverages _____

Thoughts _____

_____

_____

Date _____ Occasion _____ Location _____

Companions _____

_____

Menu _____

_____

_____

Beverages _____

Thoughts _____

_____

_____

Date _____ Occasion _____ Location _____

Companions _____

_____

Menu _____

_____

_____

Beverages _____

Thoughts _____

_____

_____

Date _____ Occasion _____ Location _____

Companions _____

_____

Menu _____

_____

_____

Beverages _____

Thoughts _____

_____

_____

Friends, Foods & Important Dates

Good manners, like good taste, derive from sensibility and simple common sense. Once mastered, that concept can be abiding and guiding. For example, it is polite to answer invitations promptly, not to wait to see if something more to your liking comes up. Similarly, it is polite to arrive on time.

—Craig Claiborne, *Elements of Etiquette*

Name _____

Contact Info: _____

Birthday/Anniversary _____

Favorite Foods _____

Favorite Beverages _____

Favorite Restaurants _____

Food Allergies & Phobias _____

Other Quirks _____

Name _____

Contact Info: _____

Birthday/Anniversary _____

Favorite Foods _____

Favorite Beverages _____

Favorite Restaurants _____

Food Allergies & Phobias _____

Other Quirks _____

Name _____

Contact Info: _____

Birthday/Anniversary _____

Favorite Foods _____

Favorite Beverages _____

Favorite Restaurants _____

Food Allergies & Phobias _____

Other Quirks _____

Name _____

Contact Info: _____

Birthday/Anniversary _____

Favorite Foods _____

Favorite Beverages _____

Favorite Restaurants _____

Food Allergies & Phobias _____

Other Quirks _____

Name _____

Contact Info: _____

Birthday/Anniversary _____

Favorite Foods _____

Favorite Beverages _____

Favorite Restaurants _____

Food Allergies & Phobias _____

Other Quirks _____

Name _____

Contact Info: _____

Birthday/Anniversary _____

Favorite Foods _____

Favorite Beverages _____

Favorite Restaurants _____

Food Allergies & Phobias _____

Other Quirks _____

Name _____

Contact Info: _____

Birthday/Anniversary _____

Favorite Foods _____

Favorite Beverages _____

Favorite Restaurants _____

Food Allergies & Phobias _____

Other Quirks _____

Name _____

Contact Info: _____

Birthday/Anniversary _____

Favorite Foods _____

Favorite Beverages _____

Favorite Restaurants _____

Food Allergies & Phobias _____

Other Quirks _____

Name _____

Contact Info: _____

Birthday/Anniversary _____

Favorite Foods _____

Favorite Beverages _____

Favorite Restaurants _____

Food Allergies & Phobias _____

Other Quirks _____

Name _____

Contact Info: _____

Birthday/Anniversary _____

Favorite Foods _____

Favorite Beverages _____

Favorite Restaurants _____

Food Allergies & Phobias _____

Other Quirks _____

Name _____

Contact Info: _____

Birthday/Anniversary _____

Favorite Foods _____

Favorite Beverages _____

Favorite Restaurants _____

Food Allergies & Phobias _____

Other Quirks _____

Name _____

Contact Info: _____

Birthday/Anniversary _____

Favorite Foods _____

Favorite Beverages _____

Favorite Restaurants _____

Food Allergies & Phobias _____

Other Quirks _____

Name _____

Contact Info: _____

Birthday/Anniversary _____

Favorite Foods _____

Favorite Beverages _____

Favorite Restaurants _____

Food Allergies & Phobias _____

Other Quirks _____

Name _____

Contact Info: _____

Birthday/Anniversary _____

Favorite Foods _____

Favorite Beverages _____

Favorite Restaurants _____

Food Allergies & Phobias _____

Other Quirks _____

Name _____

Contact Info: _____

Birthday/Anniversary _____

Favorite Foods _____

Favorite Beverages _____

Favorite Restaurants _____

Food Allergies & Phobias _____

Other Quirks _____

Name _____

Contact Info: _____

Birthday/Anniversary _____

Favorite Foods _____

Favorite Beverages _____

Favorite Restaurants _____

Food Allergies & Phobias _____

Other Quirks _____

Name _____

Contact Info: _____

Birthday/Anniversary _____

Favorite Foods _____

Favorite Beverages _____

Favorite Restaurants _____

Food Allergies & Phobias _____

Other Quirks _____

Planning

Dinner Parties • Picnics • Holiday Breakfasts • Midnight Suppers • Spring Soirées
• Harvest Feasts • Cocktail Parties

Dinner: A major daily activity, which can be accomplished in worthy fashion only by intelligent people. It is not enough to eat. To dine, there must be diversified, calm conversation. It should sparkle with the rubies of the wine between courses, be deliciously suave with the sweetness of dessert, and acquire true profundity with the coffee.

—Alexander Dumas's *Dictionary of Cuisine*

Occasion _____

Date _____ Time _____ Location _____

Guests _____

_____

_____

_____

_____

Menu _____

_____

_____

_____

_____

_____

Beverages _____

_____

_____

_____

_____

Notes _____

_____

_____

_____

_____

_____

Occasion _____

Date _____ Time _____ Location _____

Guests _____

_____

_____

_____

_____

Menu _____

_____

_____

_____

_____

_____

Beverages _____

_____

_____

_____

_____

Notes _____

_____

_____

_____

_____

_____

Occasion _____

Date _____ Time _____ Location _____

Guests _____

_____

_____

_____

_____

Menu _____

_____

_____

_____

_____

Beverages _____

_____

_____

Notes _____

Occasion _____

Date _____ Time _____ Location _____

Guests _____

Menu _____

Beverages _____

_____

_____

Notes _____

_____

_____

_____

_____

_____

Occasion _____

Date _____ Time _____ Location _____

Guests _____

_____

_____

_____

_____

Menu _____

_____

_____

_____

_____

_____

Beverages _____

_____

_____

_____

_____

Notes _____

_____

_____

_____

_____

_____

Occasion _____

Date _____ Time _____ Location _____

Guests _____

_____

_____

_____

_____

Menu _____

_____

_____

_____

_____

_____

Beverages _____

_____

_____

Notes _____

Occasion _____

Date _____ Time _____ Location _____

Guests _____

Menu _____

Beverages _____

Notes _____

Occasion _____

Date _____ Time _____ Location _____

Guests _____

Menu _____

Beverages _____

_____

_____

Notes _____

_____

_____

_____

_____

_____

Occasion _____

Date _____ Time _____ Location _____

Guests _____

_____

_____

_____

_____

Menu _____

_____

_____

_____

_____

Beverages _____

_____

_____

_____

_____

Notes _____

_____

_____

_____

_____

_____

Occasion _____

Date _____ Time _____ Location _____

Guests _____

_____

_____

_____

_____

Menu _____

_____

_____

_____

_____

_____

Beverages _____

_____

_____

Notes

Favorite Recipes

My mother and millions of American housewives like her collected recipes from newspapers and magazines. Some women attached the recipes to index cards and filed them in special plastic boxes that often matched a set of kitchen canisters. (Every now and then I stumbled over such a file box at a thrift store or estate sale; what treasures are inside!) My mother painstakingly glued hers onto white paper and placed them in a blue canvas three-ring binder that grew to two binders before I was as tall as our O'keefe and Merritt stove. Every October she would pull them out and turn to the section where she kept recipes for candies. All fall, she would make colorful fondants, divinity, all manner of fudge—the forerunner, it seems, of today's chocolate truffles—and my favorite, penuche. These pages were stained with food coloring, butter and sugar, as were the covers of the binders. Come the winter holidays, friends and neighbors received boxes full of these sweet confections and from Thanksgiving to New Year's, every guest was treated to a plateful.

A widow not long after my first birthday, my mother did not do much other cooking, at least not with joy or enthusiasm, though she still continued to fill the binder with clipped recipes, imagining, I suppose, a time in the future when she would remarry and begin to entertain again, something that never came to pass. I have no idea what happened to those thousands of recipes.

Today, some of us still clip recipes but it is much more common to search the internet, which is both convenient and infuriating. Sadly, most of the recipes posted on the internet have not been vetted and countless ones do not work. I peruse them now and then to see if they have improved and I'm always saddened by what I see, as I hate to think of home cooks giving up because they believe they can't cook when the fault is with a poorly conceived recipe that Google showed them.

That said, now and then we discover recipes that do work, especially on reliable web sites by thoughtful, conscientious cooks. I have several favorite sites, including wisekitchen.com by my friend and colleague Victoria Wise, who was the first chef at Chez Panisse back in the early 1970s. I also enjoy smittenkitchen.com, davidlebovitz.com, kimberleyhasselbrink.com (Kimberely did the photographs for my book Vinaigrettes and Other Dressings) and several others. I enjoy working on my own blogs, too, when time allows. You'll find them at pantry.blogs.pressdemocrat.com, where I organize recipes from my column Seasonal Pantry, which I've been writing since 1997, and at saladdresser.com, where I feature weekly recipes, some from my books, some from my columns and some simply inspired by the moment.

This section is designed for you to jot down the source of favorite recipes, whether web address, book titles and page numbers or what have you. You can even tuck clipped recipes from newspapers and papers between the pages.

Happy eating and *happy cooking*!

Favorite Spring Recipes

Roasted Asparagus with Poached Farm Eggs • Easter Arancine • Stinging Nettle Soup
• Grilled Apricots • Bing Cherry Salsa • Morels in Butter & Cream

RECIPE NAME	SOURCE	PAGE/WEB ADDRESS

Favorite Summer Recipes

Wild Pacific King Salmon with Salsa Verde • Insalata Caprese• White Peach Galette
• Grilled Chicken with Honey & Garlic • BLT Pasta • Strawberry Shortcake

RECIPE NAME	SOURCE	PAGE/ADDRESS

Favorite Fall Recipes

Apple Cobbler • Roasted Turkey with Sourdough Stuffing • Winter Squash Gratin
• Cranberry Kissel Grilled Lamb with Pomegranate Gremolata • Hawaiian Chile Water
• Posole Verde • Posole Rojo

RECIPE NAME	SOURCE	PAGE/ADDRESS

Favorite Winter Recipes

Spaghetti Squash Fritters • Crab Louis • Sautéed Brussels Sprout Leaves with Bacon
• Oysters on the Half Shell • Risotto with White Truffles • Steamed Persimmon Pudding
• Beignets • Prime Rib with Yorkshire Pudding

RECIPE NAME   **SOURCE**   **PAGE/ADDRESS**

Favorite Vegetable Recipes

Roasted Asparagus • Artichokes with Garlic & Olive Oil • Grilled Eggplant with Yogurt & Salsa Verde • Oven-Roasted Cauliflower • Potato-Kale Soup • Blue Lake Green Beans with Warm Tomato Vinaigrette • Winter Squash & Potato Gratin • Roasted Tomatoes & Sweet Peppers with Vinegar

RECIPE NAME	SOURCE	PAGE/ADDRESS

Favorite Poultry Recipes

Duck Meatballs • Chicken Dijonnaise • Braised Duck Legs • Seared Duck Breast
• Turkey Gumbo • Grilled Quail with Apple-Pepper Glaze • Turkey Barley Soup

RECIPE NAME	SOURCE	PAGE/ADDRESS

Favorite Meat Recipes

Barbecued Ribs • Braised Lamb Shanks • Steak Tartare • Butterflied Leg of Lamb
• Steak au Poivre Rouge • Steak au Poivre Blanc • Three Peppercorn Meatloaf

RECIPE NAME	SOURCE	PAGE/ADDRESS

Favorite Sauce Recipes

Vinaigrette • Mayonnaise • Aioli • Remoulade • Romesco • Salsa Mexicana
• Red-Eye Gravy • Alfredo • Caramel • Chermoula • Korean Barbecue Sauce

RECIPE NAME	SOURCE	PAGE/ADDRESS

Favorite Dessert Recipes

Apricot Galette • Chocolate Mousse • King Cake • Bread Pudding
• Cheesecake • Roasted Strawberries • Black Pepper Ice Cream • Sweet Rice & Mango
• Chocolate Cake with Salted Caramel Sauce

RECIPE NAME	SOURCE	PAGE/ADDRESS

Cookbooks on Loan

General • Single Subject • Ethnic • Technical • Scientific • Baking • Literary

No restaurants. The means of consoling oneself: reading cookbooks.

—Charles Baudelaire

Title _____

Author _____ Publisher _____

Loaned to _____

Email _____ Cell _____ Other _____

Title _____

Author _____ Publisher _____

Loaned to _____

Email _____ Cell _____ Other _____

Title _____

Author _____ Publisher _____

Loaned to _____

Email _____ Cell _____ Other _____

Title _____

Author _____ Publisher _____

Loaned to _____

Email _____ Cell _____ Other _____

Title _____

Author _____ Publisher _____

Loaned to _____

Email _____ Cell _____ Other _____

Title _____

Author _____ Publisher _____

Loaned to _____

Email _____ Cell _____ Other _____

Title _____

Author _____ Publisher _____

Loaned to _____

Email _____ Cell _____ Other _____

Title _____

Author _____ Publisher _____

Loaned to _____

Email _____ Cell _____ Other _____

Title _____

Author _____ Publisher _____

Loaned to _____

Email _____ Cell _____ Other _____

Title _____

Author _____ Publisher _____

Loaned to _____

Email _____ Cell _____ Other _____

Title _____

Author _____ Publisher _____

Loaned to _____

Email _____ Cell _____ Other _____

Title _____

Author _____ Publisher _____

Loaned to _____

Email _____ Cell _____ Other _____

Title _____

Author _____ Publisher _____

Loaned to _____

Email _____ Cell _____ Other _____

Title _____

Author _____ Publisher _____

Loaned to _____

Email _____ Cell _____ Other _____

Title _____

Author _____ Publisher _____

Loaned to _____

Email _____ Cell _____ Other _____

Title _____

Author _____ Publisher _____

Loaned to _____

Email _____ Cell _____ Other _____

Title _____

Author _____ Publisher _____

Loaned to _____

Email _____ Cell _____ Other _____

Title _____

Author _____ Publisher _____

Loaned to _____

Email _____ Cell _____ Other _____

Title _____

Author _____ Publisher _____

Loaned to _____

Email _____ Cell _____ Other _____

The Good Cook's Beverage Cellar

One should always be drunk. That's the great thing; the only question. Not to feel the horrible burden of Time weighing on your shoulders and bowing you to the earth, you should be drunk without respite. Drunk with what? With wine, with poetry, or with virtue, as you please. But get drunk.

—Charles Baudelaire, *Get Drunk*

When asked to speak on the topic of food and wine pairings, and on wine itself, I always remind people that any wine and any pairing is, in the end, a snapshot in time, a sum of more than just what goes into your mouth and across your palate. Everything impacts your experience, from your mood, the time of day, the weather, the slant of light, your companions and how much sleep you had the night before. It is impossible to duplicate an extraordinary experience in exactly the same way.

That said, there are wines and other beverages we want to remember. Maybe it was the experience of falling in love with pinot noir, celebrating a milestone with a special bottle or finding an inexpensive quaffer you don't want to forget. Maybe you traveled all the way from, say, Maine, to Santa Rosa, California, to stand in line for Pliny the Younger, a triple IPA that is available only at Russian River Brewing Company for just two weeks in February. Maybe you fell in love with a sour pilsner at a tiny brew pub in Park Slope.

There are many reasons to record some of the things you drink in a cellar book or something similar. Here, I give you mine. I used to tuck labels between the pages of the first edition of this book but sometime in the mid-1990s wineries began using glues that make it all but impossible to get a wine label off a bottle without damaging it. That's why, today, we use our iPhones and iPads to photograph memorable bottles.

Sparkling Wines

Champagne • Cremant • Brut • Brut Rosé • Demi-Sec • Vinho Verde • Prosecco
• Cava • Espumate • Asti • Sekt

Winery _____ Wine _____

Vintage_____Varietal _____ Appellation _____

Purchased From _____ Price _____

Tasting Notes _____

_____

Food Pairing Notes _____

_____

Champagne refers to a region, an appellation, in northern France, where méthode champenoise, the technique for producing the finest-quality sparkling wines, was developed. The bubbles in this wine are produced by carbon dioxide trapped inside a tightly corked bottle in a process that is both labor-intensive and time-consuming, hence the quality and the price of wines produced by this technique. There are quicker methods of producing sparkling wines, but they all lack the elegance and the finesse of true méthode champenoise sparkling wines.

Winery _____ Wine _____

Vintage_____Varietal _____ Appellation _____

Purchased From _____ Price _____

Tasting Notes _____

_____

Food Pairing Notes _____

_____

Winery _____ Wine _____

Vintage_____Varietal _____ Appellation _____

Purchased From _____ Price _____

Tasting Notes _____

_____

Food Pairing Notes _____

_____

Winery _____ Wine _____

Vintage_____Varietal _____ Appellation _____

Purchased From _____ Price _____

Tasting Notes _____

_____

Food Pairing Notes _____

_____

Winery _____ Wine _____

Vintage_____Varietal _____ Appellation _____

Purchased From _____ Price _____

Tasting Notes _____

_____

Food Pairing Notes _____

_____

Americans have traditionally celebrated with Champagne, but, like Europeans, we've begun to realize that a glass of bubbly has a way of making an everyday event extraordinary . . . The thrilling bubbles and luxurious taste of Champagne and sparkling wine have the power to lift our spirits, making a Tuesday-night dinner for two into a memorable celebration.

—Maria C. Hunt, *The Bubbly Bar*

Winery _____ Wine _____

Vintage_____Varietal _____ Appellation _____

Purchased From _____ Price _____

Tasting Notes _____

_____

Food Pairing Notes _____

_____

Winery _____ Wine _____

Vintage_____Varietal _____ Appellation _____

Purchased From _____ Price _____

Tasting Notes _____

_____

Food Pairing Notes _____

_____

White Wines

Chenin Blanc • Sauvignon Blanc • Pinot Grigio • Viognier • Vermentino Chardonnay • Albariño • Verdejo • Grüner Veltliner • Valpolicella • Riesling • Gewurztraminer • Traminette • White Meritage

Friends don't let friends drink chardonnay.

—Randall Graham, Bonny Doon Vineyards

Winery _____ Wine _____

Vintage_____Varietal _____ Appellation _____

Purchased From _____ Price _____

Tasting Notes _____

_____

Food Pairing Notes _____

_____

Winery _____ Wine _____

Vintage_____Varietal _____ Appellation _____

Purchased From _____ Price _____

Tasting Notes _____

_____

Food Pairing Notes _____

_____

Winery _____ Wine _____

Vintage_____Varietal _____ Appellation _____

Purchased From _____ Price _____

Tasting Notes _____

_____

Food Pairing Notes _____

_____

Winery _____ Wine _____

Vintage_____Varietal _____ Appellation _____

Purchased From _____ Price _____

Tasting Notes _____

_____

Food Pairing Notes _____

_____

Winery _____ Wine _____

Vintage_____Varietal _____ Appellation _____

Purchased From _____ Price _____

Tasting Notes _____

_____

Food Pairing Notes _____

_____

In a pinch, you can always use a wine bottle as a rolling pin.

—Laurie Colwin, *Home Cooking*

Winery _____ Wine _____

Vintage _____ Varietal _____ Appellation _____

Purchased From _____ Price _____

Tasting Notes _____

_____

Food Pairing Notes _____

_____

Winery _____ Wine _____

Vintage _____ Varietal _____ Appellation _____

Purchased From _____ Price _____

Tasting Notes _____

_____

Food Pairing Notes _____

_____

Winery _____ Wine _____

Vintage _____ Varietal _____ Appellation _____

Purchased From _____ Price _____

Tasting Notes _____

_____

Food Pairing Notes _____

_____

Rosé

From Red Grapes, Free Run Juice or Pressed Off Skins Before Fermentation

In Europe we thought of wine as something as healthy and normal as food and also as a great giver of happiness and well-being and delight. Drinking wine was not a snobbism nor a sign of sophistication nor a cult; it was as natural as eating and to me as necessary.

—Ernest Hemingway, *A Moveable Feast*

Winery _____ Wine _____

Vintage_____Varietal _____ Appellation _____

Purchased From _____ Price _____

Tasting Notes _____

_____

Food Pairing Notes _____

_____

Winery _____ Wine _____

Vintage_____Varietal _____ Appellation _____

Purchased From _____ Price _____

Tasting Notes _____

_____

Food Pairing Notes _____

_____

Winery _____ Wine _____

Vintage_____Varietal _____ Appellation _____

Purchased From _____ Price _____

Tasting Notes _____

_____

Food Pairing Notes _____

_____

Winery _____ Wine _____

Vintage_____Varietal _____ Appellation _____

Purchased From _____ Price _____

Tasting Notes _____

_____

Food Pairing Notes _____

_____

Red Wines

Pinot Noir • Syrah • Malbec • Primativo • Carignano• Cabernet Sauvignon • Zinfandel • Dolcetto • Nebbiolo• Sangiovese • Barbera • Cabernet Franc • Red Meritage • Amarone

Abstainers and heavy drinkers die sooner of all causes and are hit with crippling or lethal heart attacks at almost twice the rate as their moderately sipping neighbors.
—Lewis Perdue, *The French Paradox and Beyond*

Winery _____ Wine _____

Vintage_____Varietal _____ Appellation _____

Purchased From _____ Price _____

Tasting Notes _____

_____

Food Pairing Notes _____

_____

Winery _____ Wine _____

Vintage_____Varietal _____ Appellation _____

Purchased From _____ Price _____

Tasting Notes _____

_____

Food Pairing Notes _____

_____

Winery _____ Wine _____

Vintage_____Varietal _____ Appellation _____

Purchased From _____ Price _____

Tasting Notes _____

_____

Food Pairing Notes _____

_____

There is no money, among that which I have spent since I began to earn my living, of the expenditure of which I am less ashamed, or which gave me better value in return, than the price of the liquids chronicled in this booklet. When they were good they pleased my senses, cheered my spirits, improved my moral and intellectual powers, besides enabling me to confer the same benefit on other people.

—George Saintsbury, *Notes on a Cellar-Book*

Winery _____ Wine _____

Vintage_____Varietal _____ Appellation _____

Purchased From _____ Price _____

Tasting Notes _____

_____

Food Pairing Notes _____

_____

At their best, pinot noirs are the most romantic of wines, with so voluptuous a perfume, so sweet an edge, and so powerful a punch that, like falling in love, they make the blood run hot and the soul wax embarrassingly poetic.

—Joel Fleishman, *Vanity Fair*, August 1991

Winery _____ Wine _____

Vintage_____Varietal _____ Appellation _____

Purchased From _____ Price _____

Tasting Notes _____

_____

Food Pairing Notes _____

_____

Winery _____ Wine _____

Vintage_____Varietal _____ Appellation _____

Purchased From _____ Price _____

Tasting Notes _____

_____

Food Pairing Notes _____

_____

Pinot noir is the James Dean of wine; it's the wine women who love too much can't drink. Pinot noir is Oscar Wilde, David Janssen, Marlene Dietrich, all in your living room at the same time. Pinot noir is Cathy and Heathcliff; it's Juliet on her wedding night. It's Connie Chatterley in the rain, wearing nothing but a pair of red shoes. In its finest vintages, pinot noir is Lord Peter with Harriet in a wine-red frock.

—Michele Anna Jordan, "Sex and a Single Grape"

Dessert Wines

Late Harvest • Sweet Sparklers • Port • Sherry • Madeira

Winery _____ Wine _____

Vintage_____Varietal _____ Appellation _____

Purchased From _____ Price _____

Tasting Notes _____

_____

Food Pairing Notes _____

_____

Winery _____ Wine _____

Vintage_____Varietal _____ Appellation _____

Purchased From _____ Price _____

Tasting Notes _____

_____

Food Pairing Notes _____

_____

Winery _____ Wine _____

Vintage_____Varietal _____ Appellation _____

Purchased From _____ Price _____

Tasting Notes _____

_____

Food Pairing Notes _____

_____

Winery _____ Wine _____

Vintage _____ Varietal _____ Appellation _____

Purchased From _____ Price _____

Tasting Notes _____

_____

Food Pairing Notes _____

_____

Beer

True craft beer, those ales and lagers made by small breweries throughout America and beyond, now offer nearly as much diversity as wine. Brewmaster dinners and beer and food pairings are increasingly popular, too, and for good reason. A well-made beer is often the best match with certain foods, especially cheese. Sommeliers at high-end restaurants frequently encourage guests to try beer instead of wine with a cheese course. Cheese, one sommelier explained to me, never ever makes a wine taste better as the butterfat in the cheese prevents the wine's full expression on the palate. Beer, on the other hand, stimulates the palate in such a way that both the beverage and the cheese are enhanced. Sparkling wine and hard cider have a similar impact.

Brewery _____ Ale or Lager? _____ Style _____

Purchased From _____ Price _____

Tasting Notes _____

_____

_____

Pairing Notes _____

_____

Brewery _____ Ale or Lager? _____ Style _____

Purchased From _____ Price _____

Tasting Notes _____

_____

_____

Pairing Notes _____

_____

Brewery _____ Ale or Lager? _____ Style _____

Purchased From _____ Price _____

Tasting Notes _____

_____

_____

Pairing Notes _____

_____

Brewery _____ Ale or Lager? _____ Style _____

Purchased From _____ Price _____

Tasting Notes _____

_____

_____

Pairing Notes _____

_____

Hard Cider

John "Johnny Appleseed" Chapman did not plant trees for apple pie. The nurseryman, who was born in 1774 and passed away in 1845, planted cider apples, small, tart varieties not suitable for eating. Hard cider was once the most common beverage in America, something everyone, including children, drank because it was more wholesome than water, which was often contaminated. Hard cider all but disappeared from America for decades but has, in recent years, been making a comeback as farmers discover that it can be more profitable than selling their apples. There are now extraordinary hard ciders that are dry, sophisticated and exceptionally food friendly. Look for the best wherever apples are grown, such as Sebastopol, California, home of the beloved Gravenstein. As I write, I can see several trees outside my window, their tiny buds swelling in our early spring.

Producer _____ Style _____

Purchased From _____ Price _____

Tasting Notes _____

_____

_____

Pairing Notes _____

_____

Producer _____ Style _____

Purchased From _____ Price _____

Tasting Notes _____

_____

_____

Pairing Notes _____

_____

Producer _____ Style _____

Purchased From _____ Price _____

Tasting Notes _____

_____

_____

Pairing Notes _____

_____

Producer _____ Style _____

Purchased From _____ Price _____

Tasting Notes _____

_____

_____

Pairing Notes _____

_____

About the Author

Michele Anna Jordan has written more than twenty books about food, including the highly acclaimed *Vinaigrettes and Other Dressings* and *More Than Meatballs*, as well as the Good Cook's series. She has received numerous awards, including a James Beard Award, for her writing, her radio show, and her work as a chef. Today, she writes for the *Santa Rosa Press Democrat* and also produces and hosts *Mouthful, the Wine Country's Most Delicious Hour* on KRCB-FM.

About the Photographer

Liza Gershman is an award-winning lifestyle, food, and travel photographer whose passions have taken her to forty-five states and thirty-three countries. She is the photographer for the entire Good Cook's series. She resides in San Francisco, California.